SHIPS OF SPLENDOUR

SHIPS OF SPLENDOUR

PASSENGER LINERS IN COLOUR

WILLIAM H. MILLER

The
History
Press

Frontispiece: Together at Genoa: the *Andrea Doria*
and *Cristoforo Colombo*. (ALF Collection)

Front Cover: Il-de-France. (ALF Collection)

Back Cover: *Andrea Dorea*. (Mick Lindsay Collection)

First published 2019
This paperback edition published 2023

The History Press
97 St. George's Place, Cheltenham,
Gloucestershire GL50 3QB
www.thehistorypress.co.uk

British Library Cataloguing in Publication Data.
A catalogue record for this book is available from the British Library.

ISBN 978 1 8039 9370 6

Typesetting and origination by The History Press
Printed in Turkey by IMAK

DEDICATION

*This book is for all the great photographers of ships,
especially liners, and those who collect their work.*

FOREWORD

One of the best things about books – and especially books about one of my favourite interests: ocean liners – is just sitting in a favourite chair, turning the pages and then looking at great and different ship pictures. This book is just that: a great collection of great ship photos. Actually, it might just be one of the very best – all colour! And then what a fleet review it is!

There are most of the big and well-known liners: ships such as the *Aquitania*, *Rex*, *Normandie*, *Queen Mary*, *United States* and *France*. But there are many, many others, possibly less famous – such as the *Saturnia*, *Asama Maru*, *Stratheden*, *Olympia* and *Southern Cross*. Each of them is fascinating in their own right. I can re-read and look at the photos of these ships over and over and over.

I am also delighted to help Bill collect these photos. I like to think of myself as his first mate of sorts – Bill is, of course, the captain.

Yes, this is a special book – a unique book: all colour. I am proud to be a part of it.

Anthony La Forgia
New Jersey USA
Summer 2019

INTRODUCTION

Over the last sixty or so years, I have collected many, many photographs of ships, but mostly passenger ships. Almost all of them were views in black and white. Of course, I also had postcards in various formats: black and white, colour, and artists' renditions. I would group them by company, beginning with 'A', which included American Export Lines, American President Lines and the Anchor Line. Zim Lines came last.

But in more recent years, colour photos of ships, even some of the earliest liners, have appeared. My collection grew into the thousands, even tens of thousands. And of course, storage is different these days – from drawers and folders to computer files.

Reviewing these pictures prompted an idea: a book on bygone passenger ships but all of them in colour. Once the idea took root, I had to figure out how to organise these photos and I decided to do a fifty-year span – from 1920–70. This neatly covers the great age of the ocean liner, I thought.

I began with some of the legendary Atlantic liners, in service during the 1920s, often following heroic duties in the First World War. But I quickly moved on to other liners on other routes: to South America, Africa, Australia and the Far East. Yes, there were hundreds of ships in my initial file. Gradually, I brought the total number down to 400, then 300 and finally to about 200. Clearly, many ships were eliminated. Myself, I had some preferences and, of course, there was the quality of the photos themselves to be considered.

I have ordered the ships by the date of their completion, and in a few instances provided entries for ships that underwent a major refit or reconstruction, again ordered by date. Ships are listed with their year of completion when they need to be differentiated from another ship of the same or similar name.

Hopefully, I have created a pleasing and a varied group. It is in some ways like a large family. There are several four-stackers such as the *Mauretania* and *Olympic*, art deco trailblazer the *Île de France*, those 'flat' Italians *Saturnia* and *Vulcania* and Sweden's *Kungsholm*. There are the giants of the 1930s: the *Europa*, *Empress of Britain*, *Rex*, *Normandie* and of course the beloved Cunard 'Queens'. And some of the smaller ships such as the *Rangitiki*, *Hikawa Maru*, *Corfu* and Italy's speedy *Victoria*. Then there are the post-war years and a great array of newly built liners based on fresh designs: the *Augustus*, *Independence*, *Ryndam*, *Andrea Doria*, *Southern Cross* and of course the record-breaking *United States*. And I've included some converted and heavily refitted ships such as the *Atlantic* (a former freighter), the Greek *Arkadia* (which once had three funnels) and the *Hanseatic* (changed from three to two funnels). We finish in the 1960s, in the age of even greater change with the gradual decline of the traditional liner and the switch to sleek, all-white cruise ships. That concluding group includes the likes of the *France*, *Guglielmo Marconi*, *Michelangelo*, *Oceanic*, *Starward* and then ending with the *Queen Elizabeth 2*. What a great and diverse 'fleet'!

Myself, I can just sit and turn the pages and imagine those bygone days through these photos: those great ships sailing past, one after another, the romance of a morning arrival, a maiden voyage, a late-afternoon sailing, or a ship at night, waiting at dock. Yes, but faintly, I can almost hear those booming whistles sounding! A photographic voyage begins!

ACKNOWLEDGEMENTS

Since childhood, I have collected pictures of ships. Later, in writing books about ships, these photos have been put to use – they see 'the light of day'. They are shared. And I am especially pleased to share this group of fine, colour photos.

Otherwise, and more specifically, I must thank a large 'crew' of assistants and contributors. Special thanks to Amy Rigg for suggesting the title and The History Press for taking on the project. And very special thanks to two exceptional friends and master photo collectors: Tony La Forgia and the late Mick Lindsay. Other assistants – 'crew members' – deserving of gratitude include the late Frank Andrews, Luis Miguel Correia, Norman Knebel, the late Vincent Messina and Hisashi Noma. Further assistance came from two fine ocean-liner historians, the late Frank Braynard and the late Everett Viez. Companies and organisations that have assisted include the Cunard Line and the World Ship Society.

Any and all oversights are deeply regretted.

THE SPLENDID SHIPS

MAURETANIA

She was one of the most beloved and successful
Atlantic liners of all time – and she sailed for
twenty-seven years, from 1907–34. And then
of course, she held the coveted Blue Riband
for twenty-two years (1907–29). A near-sister
to the ill-fated *Lusitania*, the '*Maury*', as she
was dubbed, was used as a heroic troopship
during the First World War. Made over as an
all-white painted cruise ship in 1933, she was
decommissioned in September 1934 and later
sold to ship-breakers in Scotland.

AQUITANIA

Another of the Atlantic's most popular and
successful liners, the 45,647grt *Aquitania*
was also considered one of the very best
looking, both inside and out. She was even
dubbed 'the Ship Beautiful'. And notably,
she was the last of the early 'floating
palaces' and the final four-stacker. She
lasted for thirty-six years. After valiantly
serving in both world wars and making
600 crossings, she was even briefly revived
for Cunard transatlantic service in 1948–49
before being broken up in Scotland in 1950.

Gala departure: dressed in flags, the illustrious
Mauretania sails from New York's Pier 54. (Anton
Logvinenko Collection)

Above: Outbound from Southampton, the *Aquitania* makes a graceful departure. (Author's Collection)

Left: The *Aquitania* was the last liner with four funnels. She is seen here in 1949, her final year of service. (Richard Weiss Collection)

Opposite: Celebration: the very popular *Berengaria* sails between Royal Navy battleships during King George V's Silver Jubilee fleet review in June 1935. (Anton Logvinenko Collection)

BERENGARIA

One of the most famous Cunarders of all, the *Berengaria* was also immensely popular. Some loyalists in first class were said to book accommodation on-board years in advance. She had a certain personality, style and ambience that was associated with only a very few liners – the aforementioned *Mauretania* and the subsequent *Queen Mary* among them. Completed in 1913 as the Hamburg–America Line's *Imperator*, then the largest ship afloat, she was initially used on the run to New York. She later sat out the First World War before being ceded to the Americans and then the British (and sold to Cunard in 1921). In her final days, in 1938, she was tired and worn out and suffered fires.

MAJESTIC

Being the largest liner in the world in the 1920s made the *Majestic* the most popular liner on the North Atlantic. Just about everyone, it seemed, wanted to sail on the biggest ocean liner. Originally commissioned as the *Bismarck* for the Hamburg–America Line, the 56,551grt ship was not completed owing to the outbreak of war and was later ceded to Britain as part of the post-war reparations. She joined the White Star Line in 1922 as the 2,145-passenger *Majestic*. She was the world's largest liner until the arrival of the 82,799grt *Normandie* in 1935. Laid-up in 1936, she was sold for scrap but then resold to the British Admiralty and used as a cadets' training ship under the name HMS *Caledonia*. She burned and sank, however, while berthed at Rosyth, Scotland on 29 September 1939. Her remains were scrapped from 1940–43.

Above: Repairs: the world's largest liner, the *Majestic*, takes a turn in the huge graving dock at Boston. The Customs House, then the tallest building in New England, is at the right. (Author's Collection)

Opposite: The *Olympic* resting at Pier 60, New York. Another White Star liner, the *Adriatic*, is nearby, at Pier 61. (Author's Collection)

OLYMPIC

Being the sister to the immortal *Titanic* added to her fame and notoriety. Happily, however, the 882ft-long *Olympic* was destined for a far longer and more successful career. Used on the White Star Line's express service between Southampton and New York, she served mostly as a troopship during the First World War before resuming luxury service. Laid-up in 1935, she was later partly scrapped at Jarrow, England; the last remains were towed to Scotland and dismantled there.

In lay-up and her final years, the giant *Leviathan* at Pier 4, Hoboken, in 1937. (Author's Collection)

LEVIATHAN

Not all big liners had success – the 950ft-long *Leviathan* was one of the least successful and therefore least profitable liners of her time. She sailed for as few as eleven years, from 1923–34. Completed as Hamburg–America's *Vaterland* in April 1914, she was barely in German service when war started. Left at New York, she was later seized by the Americans and used as an Allied troopship. She began sailing as the *Leviathan* for the United States Lines in July 1923. Laid-up from 1934, she sailed empty to the breakers' yard at Rosyth in January 1938.

Right: One of Cunard's single-stackers of the 1920s, the 624ft-long *Samaria* takes a turn in dry dock during its winter overhaul. (Author's Collection)

PARIS

France's newest and largest liner in the early 1920s, the *Paris* quickly settled down to a very popular life. Atlantic travellers in the know often preferred her – for her on-board ambience, her fine décor and perhaps mostly for her superb kitchens. Her construction actually began in 1913, but was slowed because of the First World War. Launched in 1916, the 34,569-ton ship remained incomplete until 1921. The 764ft-long *Paris* burned and then capsized at Le Havre on 19 April 1939. The wreckage was not scrapped, however, until 1947.

SAMARIA

Cunard was feeling much more conservative following the First World War. Only moderately sized passenger ships were created, for almost twenty years. Built in 1921, the 19,602-ton *Samaria* was representative of eleven successive sister ships built in the first half of the 1920s. She carried up to 2,190 passengers and was used on the North Atlantic as well as for cruising. The *Samaria* was in fact one of the last of these single-stack Cunarders and was scrapped in 1956.

RELIANCE

She and her near-sister *Resolute* had rather varied lives, but went on to become two of the most popular cruise ships of the late 1920s and 1930s. Launched in 1913 as Hamburg–America's *Johann Heinrich Burchard*, she was sold to the Dutch, to the Royal Holland Lloyd line, in 1916 and later completed as the *Limburgia* for the Amsterdam–South America service. Unsuccessful, the 19,980-tonner was sold to the United States Lines in 1922, renamed *Reliance* and later placed under a Panamanian flag. Sold back to her original owners, Hamburg–America, in 1926, she then flew the German flag. Destroyed by fire at her Hamburg berth in August 1938, her wreckage was scrapped in 1941.

The *Stavangerfjord* of 1918 was the longest-serving of all the large Norwegian liners. (ALF Collection)

Once a four-stacker, the *Arundel Castle* was rebuilt in 1937 with two funnels, giving the ship a more contemporary appearance. (Mick Lindsay Collection)

STAVANGERFJORD

Some ships are beloved in their homelands – and the 14,015-ton *Stavangerfjord* was one of these. Sailing for some forty-five years, she was also the longest-lasting passenger liner ever to sail under the Norwegian flag. Built at Birkenhead, near Liverpool in England and commissioned in 1918, she sailed on the Oslo–New York run and escaped service in either World War. Finally retired in December 1963, she was later sold to Hong Kong scrap merchants.

ARUNDEL CASTLE

It has always been interesting that of the fourteen four-funnel liners, twelve were created for the North Atlantic and just two for another service: England–South Africa. Union–Castle Line's *Arundel Castle* and her sister, the *Windsor Castle*, were commissioned in 1921. They were for a time the biggest and finest liners on the Cape express run. But by the mid 1930s, they were looking rather dated, at least on the outside. In major refits, the four funnels came off and were replaced by two stacks, both of which had a smart rake and added to the ship's appearance. The *Arundel Castle* remained on the South-African run until 1958 and then was sold for scrapping.

GRIPSHOLM/BERLIN

When completed in 1925, the 17,993-ton *Gripsholm* garnered lots of attention – she was the very first large liner to be diesel driven. Proving very successful, she went on to be a popular Atlantic liner, successful cruise ship and, during the Second World War, a heroic diplomatic-exchange ship. And in her second career, beginning in 1955, she became the first big German liner to sail the Atlantic since 1939 and marked the return to luxury service of the illustrious North German Lloyd. As the North German Lloyd's *Berlin*, she continued in service until 1966.

BERLIN/ADMIRAL NAKHIMOV

This ship, also named *Berlin*, went on to become a popular liner under Soviet colours. But in the end, she suffered a great misfortune in one of the worst tragedies in peacetime Soviet maritime history.

Used as a hospital ship for the German navy during the Second World War, she sank after hitting a mine on 1 February 1945. Salvaged by the Soviets in 1949, she took seven years to repair and rebuild as the *Admiral Nakhimov*. Sailing mostly in the Black Sea out of Odessa, she collided with a Soviet tanker on 31 August 1986 and then sank with the loss of 423 lives.

The *Berlin*, the former *Gripsholm* of 1925, departs from New York. (ALF Collection)

Changing hands: the *Berlin* of 1925 later became the Soviet *Admiral Nakhimov*, seen here at Sochi in the Black Sea. (ALF Collection)

CONTE BIANCAMANO

One of Italy's finest liners, she had the good fortune to survive the Second World War and, in doing so, had two careers – pre- and post-war.

Built at Glasgow and completed in 1925, this 24,416-ton ship was first owned by Lloyd Sabaudo, but then transferred to the Italian Line in 1932. She served on several Italian routes – North Atlantic–South America and to the Far East. Seized by American authorities at Panama in December 1941, she was refitted as the troopship USS *Hermitage*. Returned to the Italians in 1947, she was extensively rebuilt and modernised. She endured until broken up in 1960.

CONTE GRANDE

A classic-looking liner, she, like her near-sister *Conte Biancamano*, was refitted and modernised after the War. She had a new look – sleek and more modern. In some ways, she defied her true age – coming out of the mid 1920s.

This 25,661-tonner was built for Lloyd Sabaudo, but transferred to the Italian Line in 1932. Used on both the Italy–New York and South America services, she was seized by the Brazilian Government at Santos in 1940 and later transferred to the US government and used as the troopship USS *Monticello*. Returned to the Italians in 1947, she was thoroughly rebuilt and in service until scrapped in 1961.

Opposite: Modern look: rebuilt and modernised after the the Second World War, the handsome *Conte Biancamano* is seen here at the Commonwealth Pier, Boston in 1950. (ALF Collection)

Right: Mighty Italian: the *Conte Grande* seen in her original Lloyd Sabaudo colours. (ALF Collection)

Migrants to South America: the Hamburg–South America Line's *Monte Pascoal* seen in Hamburg harbour. (ALF Collection)

MONTE PASCOAL

There was considerable migration between Europe and South America in the years between the wars. Among others, Germany's Hamburg–South America Line realised this and built a series of primarily low-fare passenger ships specifically for this service.

There were five liners in this class and the 13,870-ton *Monte Pascoal* was the fourth. Completed in 1931, she had quarters for some 2,400 passengers – 1,400 in tourist class and 1,000 in steerage. Initially used on the Hamburg–Rio de Janeiro–Buenos Aires run, she was later used as an accommodation ship for the German navy during much of the Second World War. She burned, however, during an Allied air attack in February 1944. Later salvaged, the 524ft-long ship was seized by the British in May 1945, but deemed unworthy of further use. Loaded with Nazi chemical-warfare materials, she was deliberately sunk by the Royal Navy on 31 December 1946.

ASTURIAS

Owned by Britain's Royal Mail Lines, she and her sister *Alcantara* were among the very finest liners on the South Atlantic run, from England to the east coast of South America. Refitted as an armed merchant cruiser for duties in the Second World War, the 1,410-passenger *Asturias* was torpedoed by an Italian submarine on 25 July 1943. Later beached at Freetown, she was initially declared a complete loss, but then reappraised and salvaged in 1945. Later rebuilt but with only one instead of two funnels, she was used as a peacetime troopship and migrant ship.

Still in wartime grey but with a Royal Mail Lines' yellow funnel, the *Asturias* is seen at Melbourne in a photo dated 17 November 1946. (Anton Logvinenko Collection)

MALOLO/QUEEN FREDERICA

After surviving a serious collision during her sea trials, this ship was responsible for an upsurge in tourism to the Hawaiian Islands. And later, in a career that spanned some fifty years, she successfully served other owners on a variety of passenger services.

Built for the Matson Line's San Francisco–Honolulu service, carrying up to 693 all first-class passengers, the 17,232grt *Malolo* was refitted in 1937 and renamed *Matsonia*. Used as a troopship in the period 1942–46, she resumed Hawaiian services from 1946–48. Sold to the Home Lines and raising the Panamanian flag in 1948, she was renamed *Atlantic* for transatlantic service. Sold again in 1954, to the National Hellenic American Line (Greek flag), she was renamed *Queen Frederica*. Sold yet again, in 1965, to the Chandris Line (also Greek), she ran Atlantic crossings as well as Australian and around-the-world sailings. Last used as a cruise ship from 1970–73, she was laid up until catching fire when being scrapped in 1978. Her remains were later demolished.

ÎLE DE FRANCE

One of the most important and innovative liners of all, this ship was perhaps mostly noted for its décor. She introduced art deco to the high seas – a style soon copied and used by other owners for their ships.

This 43,153-tonner, completed in 1927, was hugely popular on the Le Havre–New York run. Serving as an Allied troopship from 1940–46, the *Île de France* was restored as a passenger liner during a two-year refit from 1947–49. In the process, her original three funnels were replaced with two of more contemporary design.

Above right: Pacific waters: the Matson Line's *Malolo*, completed in 1927, did much to increase tourism to Hawaii. (ALF Collection)

Below right: Morning arrival: several tugs dock the innovative *Île de France* at New York's Pier 57. (ALF Collection)

Well-wishers: the *Saturnia* makes a noontime departure from New York's
Pier 84 in a view from 1955. (ALF Collection)

Off on a cruise: the all-white *Caribia*, the former *Vulcania*, is seen
departing from Genoa. A fleetmate, the *Irpinia*, can be seen at the far left.
(Mick Lindsay Collection)

SATURINA

Seemingly flat with her squat funnel, this Italian motor liner appeared longer than it was. Built at Monfalcone, Italy for the Cosulich Line (Italian flag) in 1927, this 23,940-tonner could carry up to 2,197 passengers in four classes. Used on the Trieste–Venice–New York run, she was later transferred to the Italian Line and then briefly used during the Second World War as an International Red Cross evacuation ship. Seized by the Americans in 1943, she became a troopship and then briefly a hospital ship, the USS *Frances Y Slanger*. Returned to the Italians in 1946, the 632ft-long ship resumed Mediterranean–New York service until broken up in 1965.

VULCANIA/CARIBIA

A close sister to the *Saturnia*, the *Vulcania* had an even longer life – sailing for almost fifty years. Completed in 1928 for the Cosulich Line (and later used by the Italian Line), she too became an International Red Cross evacuation ship in 1942, and then a US-operated troopship in 1943. Returned to the Italian Line in 1947, she later resumed Mediterranean–New York service. Sold to the Siosa Lines (also Italian) in 1965, she was renamed *Caribia* and used first on the Southampton–Caribbean service and later for cruising only. Her final days were somewhat complicated. Grounded off Nice on 23 September 1972, she was too old to repair and so was sold to Spanish ship-breakers in 1973, but then resold to Taiwanese scrappers in 1974. Towed to the Far East, she sank in Kaohsiung harbour in Taiwan on 20 July 1974. She was later refloated and finally scrapped.

KUNGSHOLM/ITALIA (1928)

Sweden's flagship, this ship had careers as both an Atlantic liner and a popular cruise ship. And following the Second World War, she did the same but for other owners. Success and profitability – and popularity – remained with her.

Warm waters: the *Italia*, the former *Kungsholm* of 1928, is seen at anchor off Nassau. (Author's Collection)

Built at Hamburg and completed in 1928, this 20,223-ton liner was sold to the US Government in 1942, and became the troopship USS *John Ericsson*. Damaged by fire at New York in 1947, she was resold to her original owners, the Swedish American Line, but then promptly sold again to the Home Lines (Panamanian flag) and refitted as the *Italia*. Used for Italy–South America and later North Atlantic services to New York and to Montreal, she was used as a full-time cruise ship from 1960–64. Sold to Bahamian interests in 1964, she became the moored floating hotel *Imperial Bahama Hotel* at Freeport. Unsuccessful in this role, she was sold to Spanish ship-breakers a year later.

STATENDAM

The great Holland–America Line opted to be rather traditionalist – they created a three-funnel Atlantic liner at the very end of the 1920s and, avoiding new, sleek art deco, used very traditional interior décor.

The twin-funnel *Orontes* lying in London Docks. (Mick Lindsay Collection)

Built as the new Dutch flagship, the 29,511-ton *Statendam's* creation was quite extended. She was laid down (at Belfast) in 1921, but the launching was delayed until 1924; then the incomplete ship was towed to Holland in 1927; it was finally finished in 1929. Used on the Rotterdam–New York run and for cruising, she was bombed and burned-out during the Nazi invasion of Rotterdam on 11–14 May 1940. Her wreckage was scrapped later that same year.

ORONTES

To reinforce its position on the long-haul UK–Australia run, the London-based Orient Line added a series of five twin-funnel liners that were among the finest and largest of their time in the industry down under.

Built by Vickers at Barrow, the 664ft-long *Orontes* was the last of these five when completed in the summer of 1929. Used on the London–Suez–Melbourne–Sydney run, she had accommodation for 500 passengers in first class and some 1,112 in third class. Used as an Allied troopship during the Second World War, she resumed Australian service in 1948 until broken up in Spain in 1962.

On the Pacific run: Japan's smart-looking *Asama Maru* of 1929. (ALF Collection)

ASAMA MARU

The NYK Line, Nippon Yusen Kaisha, operated the biggest and finest liners under the Japanese flag on the trans-Pacific run between the Far East and the United States. Built by Mitsubishi at Nagasaki, this 16,975-tonner could carry up to 822 passengers in three classes. Commissioned in 1929, the *Asama Maru* was used as a Japanese troopship from 1941–44. She was sunk by an American submarine in the China Sea on 1 November 1944. Earlier, in September 1937, the ship was driven aground by a fierce hurricane at Hong Kong. The salvage process was intense – over 3,500 tons of material including two of the four main engines had to be removed to lighten the ship and refloat it. In all, the *Asama Maru* was out of service for a year.

RANGITATA/RANGITIKI/RANGITOTO

All these ships were large passenger–cargo liners, deriving their income not only from some 600 passengers, but also from freight carried in seven holds. Along with regular passengers including occasional tourists, they carried British manufactured goods on their outward sailings to New Zealand and returned with large amounts of meat and wool.

Built on the Clyde, the *Rangitata* of 1929 and her two sisters belonged to the New Zealand Shipping Company and flew the British flag. Used on the long-haul run via Panama between London, Auckland and Wellington, the *Rangitata* had 33 years of service before being scrapped in 1962.

Sentimental journey: the *Rangitiki* on her final visit to London in 1962. (Mick Lindsay Collection)

On the run to Canada: the *Empress of France* at Liverpool. (Mick Lindsay Collection)

BREMEN (1929)

The flagship of the German and later Nazi-German fleet, the mighty *Bremen* found herself at New York just days before the Second World War started in Europe, on 1 September 1939. It was an unfortunate miscalculation, but Hitler himself insisted that she return to home waters.

Built at Bremen, this 51,656-ton liner was built for North German Lloyd's Bremerhaven–New York express service and was completed in the summer of 1929. She captured the Blue Riband for a year and then briefly regained it in 1933. After returning to Bremerhaven in late 1939, she was idle until destroyed by fire on 16 March 1941. Completely ruined, her wreckage was later scrapped and her last remains were sunk in the River Weser.

EUROPA (1930)

A near-sister to the aforementioned *Bremen*, both liners achieved great acclaim by winning the Blue Riband for record Atlantic passages. But the *Europa* had a close call: she was nearly destroyed while still incomplete, in March 1929, and might have been scrapped. She was repaired, however, but delayed by over a year. She was laid-up at Bremerhaven in September 1939 and remained there until seized by American invasion forces in May 1945. Briefly used as the troopship USS *Europa*, she was plagued with fires and given over to the French in 1946 as part of the German reparations. Renamed *Liberté*, she was nearly lost a second time after sinking at her Le Havre berth in December 1946. Salvaged and finally restored, she entered French Line transatlantic service in August 1950.

DUCHESS OF BEDFORD/EMPRESS OF FRANCE

They were known to be rather unsteady at sea and so were dubbed the 'Drunken Duchesses'. Canadian Pacific Steamships built four of them for summer-season service on the North Atlantic; they spent the rest of the year cruising. Built in 1928–29, they were named *Duchess of Atholl*, *Duchess of Bedford*, *Duchess of Richmond* and *Duchess of York*.

Built on the Clyde by John Brown & Co., the 20,123-ton *Duchess of Bedford* lasted the longest. After serving as a troopship from 1939–47, she was refitted as the *Empress of France*. Resuming transatlantic service to Canada, she was (at thirty-three) scrapped in Wales in 1961.

EMPRESS OF JAPAN/SCOTLAND

Canadian Pacific Steamships maintained two major liner services: transatlantic and trans-Pacific. On the Pacific side, their Empress liners were big, well run and popular. To reinforce this service, by the late 1920s, the company ordered the biggest Pacific Empress yet – the superb *Empress of Japan*. And she earned further acclaim: she became the fastest liner in Pacific service.

Final call: the *Bremen* at New York in August 1939, on the German flagship's last visit to New York. (ALF Collection)

Opposite and right: Two identities: the mighty *Europa* had a German career in the 1930s and a French phase in the 1950s.
In the picture on the right, the *Europa* is approaching Pier 86 at New York with the Hamburg–America Line's *Deutschland* in the lower left (ALF Collection)

Above: Wartime at Wellington. The *Empress of Japan* (left) and the *Mauretania* in a photo dated 1940 (ALF Collection)

Opposite above: New York arrival: the *Britannic* is berthed at Pier 92 and is seen from the arriving *Queen Mary*. (ALF Collection)

Opposite centre: Museum ship: the *Hikawa Maru* is seen at Yokohama in a view dated July 1978. (Author's Collection)

Opposite below: The *Empress of Britain* seen in the River Clyde, bound for its sea trials. (Anton Logvinenko Collection)

Built at Glasgow, this 26,000-tonner served as a troopship (1939–48) and was renamed *Empress of Scotland* in 1942. Resuming Canadian Pacific service in 1950, but on the North Atlantic run, she was sold in 1957 to the Hamburg–Atlantic Line (West German flag) and renamed *Hanseatic* (q.v.).

BRITANNIC

Although financially ailing, Britain's White Star Line was hoping to build a super liner, the 60,000-ton *Oceanic*, in the late 1920s. It was even said such a big ship would be the consort, the running mate, to a super liner being planned by Cunard. But White Star's order was soon modified – the big liner project was dropped and replaced by two medium-sized, more sensible liners: the 27,000-ton near-sisters *Britannic* and *Georgic*.

HIKAWA MARU

A rather small, workaday Japanese passenger ship, she survived the Second World War and became the country's only passenger ship in Pacific service in the 1950s. Since 1960, she has been a moored museum and accommodation ship in Yokohama harbour.

EMPRESS OF BRITAIN

She was one of the greatest, grandest and in many ways most glamorous liners of the 1930s. She was also the biggest ever for Canadian Pacific Steamships, and the fastest to sail on the Canadian run. She was also dual-purpose: crossings in the summer, luxury cruises for the rest of the year.

Completed in 1931, this 42,348-ton liner could carry 1,195 passengers in three classes or 700 all first-class for cruises. She became a troopship in late 1939, but it was short-lived – she was attacked by German bombers off the Irish coast on 26 October 1940 and then was torpedoed two days later by a German submarine. Forty-nine people perished.

CORFU

Overseas colonies provided work for many passenger ships, which transported passengers, freight and mail between the motherland and distant outposts. For service to faraway Singapore and Hong Kong, the P&O Lines added two sister ships, the *Corfu* and *Carthage* in 1931.

STRATHAIRD

For its more important liner service to Australia, P&O added two fine liners in 1931–32. Painted in all-white (a first for P&O), they were intended to be authentic ocean liners. They were even fitted with three funnels, long reasoned to be reminders of the great Atlantic liners. Two of the funnels were in fact dummies. And, beginning in 1932, these 'Strath' liners introduced cruising from Australia and with Australian passengers. Today, Australia is one of the fastest growing cruise markets in the world.

PRESIDENT HOOVER

American shipowners, never highly interested in big passenger ships, went on a building boom in the late 1920s and early 1930s. The Panama Pacific Line created three 20,000-ton liners for trans-Panama Canal service, linking both coasts; then the Matson Line ordered three large ships for Pacific sailings; and the Dollar Line built two major ships for trans-Pacific service.

Completed in 1931, the 21,936-ton *President Hoover* was one of the Dollar Line ships and could carry nearly 1,000 passengers, divided in three classes. Crossing to the likes of Yokohama, Hong Kong and Shanghai, her career was sadly very short – the 654ft liner struck a reef in Japanese waters on 10 December 1937 and was wrecked. Her remains were later scrapped on the spot.

Above right: The *Corfu* being shifted in London Docks – with the *Dominion Monarch* in the lower right. (Mick Lindsay Collection)

Below right: The *Strathnaver* and her sister *Strathaird* introduced white hull colouring to the P&O fleet in 1931–32. (ALF Collection)

Opposite: Overhaul: the *Empress of Britain* entering the big floating dock at Southampton. (ALF Collection)

The *President Hoover* berthed at Los Angeles. (ALF Collection)

VICTORIA (1931)

She was often appraised as the finest liner in Europe–Far East service. And she was also the fastest. The late ship historian and author Frank O. Braynard said she was like 'an Italian yacht'. Owned by the Trieste-based Lloyd Triestino line, the 13,000-ton *Victoria* was commissioned in 1931 and used on the long-haul run between Genoa–Bombay–Hong Kong–Shanghai. Diesel-driven, she was a fast ship, making up to 23 knots on her trials. Used as a troopship by the Italian navy during the Second World War, she was bombed and sunk by British aircraft while in the Mediterranean on 24 January 1942.

CHAMPLAIN

Several ocean liner historians agree that she was a prelude to the far larger, far grander *Normandie*. The two ships were three years apart. The 28,124-ton *Champlain* entered service in June 1932. Used on the Le Havre–New York run as well as for cruising, she was an early casualty of the Second World War, having struck a mine and then sinking off western France on 17 June 1940. Some 330 perished. Her wreckage lingered: it took eighteen years to scrap her, from 1946–64.

Above: Bound for Shanghai: the handsome, yacht-like *Victoria* of Lloyd Triestino. (ALF Collection)

Below: In a photo dated September 1939, the *Champlain* is being repainted in wartime grey. The funnels of the *Normandie* can be seen on the far side of Pier 88 and a floating crane is loading military equipment on-board. (ALF Collection)

GEORGIC

This liner, the last for the White Star Line, was completed in 1932. A 27,759-ton liner, she was used on the Liverpool–New York run and for cruising. A near-sister to the aforementioned *Britannic*, the *Georgic* became a troopship in 1940. She was badly damaged by German bombers at Port Tewfik, Egypt on 14 July 1941. A long salvage and repair process followed, lasting over three years (1941–44). Rebuilt as a full-time troopship, after the war she also served as a migrant ship and seasonal passenger ship for Cunard (1950–55). She was scrapped in 1956.

REX

She was Italy's finest liner between the wars and also their fastest – a Blue Riband champion. But unfortunately, she sailed for only eight years and was then destroyed in the dark days of the Second World War.

Originally intended to be called *Dux* and possibly *Guglielmo Marconi*, the 51,062-ton *Rex* was the flagship of Italian's Italy–New York service. She could carry up to 2,358 passengers (in four classes) and made the run between Naples and New York in 9 days. Being the world's fastest liner from 1933–35 added to her popularity. Laid-up in June 1940, she was 'hidden' in an anchorage near Trieste, but was bombed and set afire by British aircraft on 8 September 1944. Her remains were scrapped over several years from 1947–58.

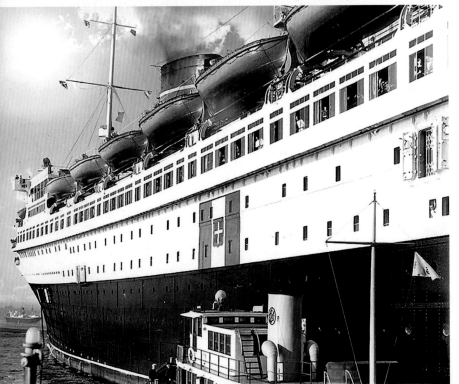

Above left: New York's Luxury Liner Row includes the *Georgic* in this view from March 1937 – (from left to right) *Europa, Rex, Normandie, Georgic* and *Berengaria*. (Anton Logvinenko Collection)

Below left: The mighty *Rex* in New York's Lower Bay in a scene dated April 1940. Note the liner's neutrality markings. (ALF Collection)

CONTE DI SAVOIA

Another great Italian liner, she also had a far too short a life and was heavily damaged in the war years. But it is interesting to contemplate that she might have been repaired, restored and used in Italian service. Other possibilities included being sold and rebuilt for the French Line or for the Holland–America Line. But none of those plans ever came to pass.

Like the *Rex*, she was completed in 1932, but this 48,502grt liner was noted for her fine exterior profile and some of her interior fittings and décor. She too served on the Italy–New York run until laid-up in mid 1940. She was set afire and partly sunk near Venice on 11 September 1943. The wreckage was raised and later scrapped, from 1945–50.

MARIPOSA/HOMERIC

The San Francisco-headquartered Matson Line created a trio of passenger liners in 1931–32 – *Lurline*, *Mariposa* and *Monterey* – which became three of the most enduring, well-used passenger ships ever. The *Monterey* alone endured for sixty-one years.

Above: Night-time lights: the *Conte di Savoia* at Genoa. (ALF Collection)

Below: Bon voyage: the *Mariposa* departing from San Francisco. (ALF Collection)

The first of this trio, the 18,000-ton, 700-passenger *Mariposa*, was completed in late 1931 and then used on Matson's San Francisco–South Pacific–Australia service. Serving as a troopship from 1941–46, she was not restored but laid-up from 1946–53. Sold in 1953 to the Home Lines (Panamanian flag) and refitted as their *Homeric*, she sailed as a transatlantic liner and winter cruise ship. She was damaged by fire off New Jersey on 1 July 1973, declared too old to repair and then scrapped in Taiwan in 1974.

MONTEREY/MATSONIA/LURLINE/BRITANIS

This ship of many names had an exceptional career – 61 years in all. Having been built for Matson's South Pacific service and serving as a troopship from 1941–46, she too was laid-up from 1946–56 owing to the high cost of restoration. She was, however, refitted and modernised as the *Matsonia*; as such, she resumed Matson service in 1957. Renamed *Lurline* in 1963, she was sold to the Chandris Lines (Greek flag) in 1970 and was rebuilt as their *Britanis*. Used as a full-time cruise ship from 1975 onwards, she was finally retired by Chandris in 1995, but then served for a time as an accommodation ship in Cuba. Sold in 1998, she was renamed *Belophin I*, but remained laid-up. While en route to Indian scrappers, empty and under tow, the ship sank off South Africa on 21 October 2000.

LURLINE

The last of the Matson trio, the 632ft-long *Lurline* was created specifically for the San Francisco–Honolulu service. As built, she could carry up to 800 passengers – 550 in first class and 250 in second class. Used as a troopship during the Second World War, she resumed Hawaiian service from 1948–63 and then was sold to the Chandris Lines (Greek flag), becoming the *Ellinis*. Her capacity was increased: in fact, more than doubled – to 1,668. Used mostly on the Europe–Australia service, she was laid-up from 1980–87 and then scrapped in Taiwan.

Hawaiian voyages: the very popular *Lurline* is seen at Honolulu in a view from atop the Aloha Tower. (ALF Collection)

Above: End of her days: The *Homeric* is laid-up at Genoa, soon to be sold to breakers. The *Stelvio* (left) and cruise ship *Caribia 2* are also seen. (Author's Collection)

SANTA ROSA (1932)

The New York-based Grace Line built a quartet of four, fine-looking, smallish passenger ships for Caribbean–South America services from New York as well as the US West Coast. Topped by twin funnels (and in this respect a prelude to the later *America* and still later the *United States*), they were constructed quite close to New York, their homeport, at the Federal Shipbuilding & Dry Dock Co. yard at Kearney, New Jersey.

The two ships of this class that survived the Second World War, the 9,000-ton sisters *Santa Rosa* and *Santa Paula*, resumed New York–Caribbean service until replaced in 1958. Both went on to further careers, but under the Greek flag and for Typaldos Lines as the cruise ships *Acropolis* and *Athinai* respectively.

QUEEN OF BERMUDA

She was one of the most popular liners ever – and was even dubbed 'the honeymoon ship', for her six-day cruises between New York and Bermuda. She also had the distinction of having had one, two and three funnels during her career – three as built, two during the Second World War, and one after being rebuilt in 1962. This 580ft-long liner endured for thirty-three years, from 1933 until scrapped in 1966.

Above right: The *Santa Rosa* and her three original sisters were designed for service to Caribbean and South American ports. (ALF Collection)

Below right: Saturday-afternoon sailing: the beautiful *Queen of Bermuda* sails from New York's Pier 95. (ALF Collection)

NORMANDIE

Big, fast, innovative and almost overly luxurious, France's extraordinary *Normandie* was a trendsetter, an inspiration and always newsworthy. But she was also something of a femme fatale – she had her tragedies. Very sadly, she only sailed for four years and then, carelessly, was destroyed during the Second World War. When barely more than ten years old, her ruined remains were sold for demolition. A great tragedy!

Completed for the French Line in the spring of 1935, she took the Blue Riband from Italy's *Rex*. A year later, she lost it to Britain's *Queen Mary*. The *Normandie* regained the pennant in 1937, but then lost it again to the *Queen Mary* in 1938. Used on the Le Havre–New York express run, she was laid-up at New York in August 1939; seized by US authorities in December 1941; and then renamed USS *Lafayette*. Conversion began to a 15,000-troop capacity transport when she caught fire and then capsized at her New York pier on 9–10 February 1942. She was later salvaged and then broken up from 1946–47 at Port Newark, New Jersey.

Festive occasion: the *Normandie* prepares to sail from Pier 88. (ALF Collection)

Top left: The *Normandie* at Le Havre – with the *Champlain* at the far left. Note the sleek, art deco clock and tidal tower in the centre. (ALF Collection)

Top right: The extraordinary *Normandie* resting between voyages to New York at her Le Havre berth. (ALF Collection)

Left: Dockside at Le Havre – the *Île de France* is just behind the mighty *Normandie*. (ALF Collection)

Tragedy: the magnificent *Normandie* capsized at Pier 88, New York, already partially demolished. This view dates from March 1942. (ALF Collection)

Skilful handling: the majestic *Queen Mary* approaches Pier 90 in a scene dated December 1948. (ALF Collection)

QUEEN MARY

This great ship was also one of the most successful, most heroic and most beloved. Passengers and crew alike just loved, even adored, the *Queen Mary*.

Built for the Cunard–White Star Line and commissioned in the spring of 1936, the 81,235-ton, 1,018ft-long liner was used on the express run between Southampton, Cherbourg and New York. Britain's largest liner, she was also the world's fastest ship from 1938–52. Serving as a heroic troopship from 1940–46, she carried some 1 million military passengers. Resuming Atlantic service from 1947 through to 1967, she was the last three-funnel liner when retired. Afterward, she was sold to the City of Long Beach, California and refitted from 1967–71 as a museum, hotel and convention centre.

ORION

Competition – often keen – has always been part of the shipping business. Every line wanted newer, larger, faster, more luxurious and more innovative ships than its rivals. Wanting to strengthen its UK–Australia run, Britain's Orient Line added two significant liners in the mid 1930s: the close sisters *Orion* and *Orcades*. Commissioned in 1935, the 1,139-passenger *Orion* introduced the first art deco décor on the down under run. She was quickly judged to be a sensation – and she served as a lone reminder for the Australians of the famed, deco-decorated transatlantic liners.

Above: Three funnels: the *Queen Mary* departing from Southampton. (ALF Collection)

Below: Handling the liners: the *Orion* arriving in London Docks – with P&O's *Canton* on the left. (Mick Lindsay Collection)

Above: Arriving from Sydney: the *Stratheden* arrives at London. (Mick Lindsay Collection)

Below: Long and sleek: the *Stirling Castle* at Southampton. (Mick Lindsay Collection)

STRATHEDEN

On the same Australian service, P&O deployed its series of Strath liners, using the slightly larger and fancier pair – the sisters *Stratheden* and *Strathallan*. While the latter ship was a casualty of war, the *Stratheden* – commissioned in 1937 – continued on the Australian run until 1964. She was then sold to the Latsis Line (Greek flag) and was renamed *Henrietta Latsi*, being used for Muslim pilgrim voyages and as a moored hotel at Jeddah. Renamed *Marianna Latsi* in 1966, she was scrapped in Italy in 1969.

STIRLING CASTLE

Britain's Union–Castle retained dominance on the Southampton–Cape Town–Durban express mail run with increasingly larger liners. The 25,550-ton sisters *Athlone Castle* and *Stirling Castle* were added in 1935–36. Along with quarters for 789 passengers in two classes, these ships also had enormous cargo capacities.

PILSUDSKI

Poland wanted a greater share of the transatlantic passenger trade and so reached an agreement, in 1934, with an Italian shipyard to build two medium-sized liners: the sister ships *Pilsudski* and *Batory*. Smart-looking ships, they were unique in being paid for in shipments of Polish coal sent to Italy. Wartime can be hideously and cruelly destructive and the Second World War was no exception. The 14,294-ton *Pilsudski* had a very short life, lasting only four years. Completed in 1935, she struck a German mine off the River Humber and then sank on 26 November 1939.

BATORY

The *Pilsudski's* sister ship, the *Batory*, had a long, useful life by comparison. Completed in 1936 and later used as an Allied troopship, she served on the North Atlantic and also North Europe–Middle East passenger trades. Retired in 1969, she became a hotel ship at Gdynia, but this venture proved unsuccessful and two years later the 526ft-long liner was sold to Hong Kong scrap merchants.

Above: Summer cruising: at anchor, the *Pilsudski* is on the right, in this view of Stockholm harbour. The *Kungsholm* is on the left; the *Stella Polaris* in the centre. (ALF Collection)

Below: Serving her owners: the popular *Batory* had a career that spanned thirty-three years. (Mick Lindsay Collection)

Among the most beautiful liners of the 1930s, the second funnel aboard the *Nieuw Amsterdam* was actually a dummy. (ALF Collection)

NIEUW AMSTERDAM

Apart from being a superbly designed and decorated liner, she was the 'Darling of the Dutch' following liberation from Nazi invasion in 1945. The 758ft-long *Nieuw Amsterdam* returned triumphantly to Rotterdam in April 1946 and became a symbol of freedom and revival. Completed in May 1938, she quickly became one of the most popular liners on the Atlantic trade between Rotterdam and New York. This great popularity continued after her war years as a hard-worked troop transport and made the 36,287grt, 1,220-passenger ship one of the most successful of all. She sailed until 1974.

Below left: Another summer cruise: the *Nieuw Amsterdam* anchored in Norway's Geirangerfjord in a view from 1972. (Vincent Messina Collection)

Below right: Preparing to sail from New York's Pier 40, the twin funnels of the *Nieuw Amsterdam* make an impressive sight. (ALF Collection)

DOMINION MONARCH

Completed in 1939, just months before the start of the Second World War, this 27,155-ton ship was actually a very large passenger–cargo ship. Her capacity was limited to 517, all first class. Used as a troopship during the war, she resumed UK–South Africa–Australia–New Zealand service until 1962. She was considered by many to be one of the finest passenger ships on the Australian run. She was used as a hotel ship for the Seattle World's Fair of 1962, and after that stint was broken up later that same year but as the *Dominion Monarch Maru*.

Right: The *Dominion Monarch* in her final days – being used as a floating hotel at Seattle in a view dated June 1962. (ALF Collection)

ANDES

By 1939, Britain's Royal Mail Lines hoped to reinforce its luxury service to the east coast of South America with a new flagship. Named *Andes*, she was commissioned in September 1939, but war suddenly broke out – there was no gala maiden voyage. Instead, the ship was soon painted in all-grey and pressed into military duty, ferrying troops all over the world. After finally entering liner service in 1948, she was made over as a full-time cruise ship in 1959–60. She then had a very popular second career until she retired in 1971.

Opposite: South America bound: the *Andes* calls at Cherbourg during a regular Southampton–Buenos Aires voyage. (Anton Logvinenko Collection)

Above: Beginning in 1960, the *Andes* was repainted in all-white and used only for cruising. To some, she resembled a 'big yacht'. (Mick Lindsay Collection)

Far East voyages: P&O's *Canton* at London, between voyages out to Eastern ports. (Mick Lindsay Collection)

CANTON

On its Far East run, to Singapore, Hong Kong and other ports, P&O added another new liner, the 480-passenger *Canton*, in 1939. This 15,784grt ship carried cargo as well as passengers between London, Suez, and ports in the Far East.

MAURETANIA (1939)

Between building the *Queen Mary* and the *Queen Elizabeth*, Cunard wanted a third big liner, but not quite as big or as fast as the two Queens. Built by Cammell Laird at Birkenhead, and completed in June 1939, she was given an illustrious Cunard name: *Mauretania*. She would go on to become one of that company's most successful liners.

Bon voyage: the *Mauretania* departing from New York. (Author's Collection)

Repainted in green in her final years and used mostly for cruising, the *Mauretania* is seen on a winter's day at Pier 90. (ALF Collection)

At Pier 92 in New York, the *Mauretania* is seen from the soon-to-depart *Queen Mary*. (ALF Collection)

ORANJE

Dutch colonial service out to the East Indies, to ports such as Bali, Surabaya and Batavia, was dominated by two shipping lines: the Nederland Line and Rotterdam Lloyd. By the late 1930s, both companies were planning their biggest and best liners yet. For Nederland, it was the 20,000grt *Oranje*, named by HM Queen Wilhelmina and honouring the royal house of Orange. Carrying up to 717 passengers in four classes, she served as a hospital ship during the Second World War, but then resumed Dutch liner service from 1946–64. Later sold to the Italian Lauro Line, she then had a successful life as the *Angelina Lauro* (q.v.).

PANAMA

'They were almost like railway passenger cars – they were sleek, shiny, very streamlined in places', remarked Frank O. Braynard. Panama Line, whose ships sailed under a US flag, built three, quite remarkable passenger–cargo liners in 1939 for their New York–Panama Canal service. These 216-berth ships were named *Panama*, *Ancon* and *Cristobal*. Each was a superb example of art deco interior design.

PATRIA

Built for Hamburg–America Line's service to the west coast of South America from Hamburg, the 598ft-long *Patria* was added in 1939, but went on to survive the war. She even served for a short time as the seat of the Nazi government, before its dissolution after Germany's surrender in May 1945. Soon afterwards and having been seized by the British, she was renamed *Empire Welland*. A year later, she was allocated to the Soviets and became the *Rossia*, mostly for Black Sea service out of Odessa. She sailed to the breakers in Pakistan as the temporarily renamed *Aniva* in 1985.

Above left: A sleek combo ship: the *Panama* arriving at Cristobal. (ALF Collection)

Below left: During a 1939 summer cruise, the *Patria* is berthed at Copenhagen. (ALF Collection)

PASTEUR

Built for the Compagnie Sud-Atlantique, this 29,253-ton liner was intended to be France's finest on the South Atlantic run to the east coast of South America. Her intended maiden voyage was set for September 1939, but was cancelled when war broke out, and instead the 751-passenger ship was made over as a 4,000-capacity troopship. She remained in troop service until 1957, until sold to the North German Lloyd line to become the 'new' *Bremen* (q.v.).

Duty overseas: troops on the French *Pasteur*.
(ALF Collection)

Winter's day: the *America* is berthed at the Columbus Quay at Bremerhaven. (ALF Collection)

AMERICA

This 33,500-ton liner was the ultimate American passenger ship when she was completed in the summer of 1940. But her intended North Atlantic service had to be postponed owing to the outbreak of war in Europe. Briefly used as a cruise ship, she became the troopship USS *West Point* in 1941. Reverting to her original name in 1946, she remained on the Atlantic run until 1964 and then was sold to the Chandris Lines (Greek flag), becoming the *Australis*. Used on the around-the-world trade, she was sold and renamed *America* in 1978 for cruising from New York. Proving unsuccessful, she was resold back to Chandris, renamed *Italis* and used for further cruising. Laid-up, however, from 1979, she was again sold and renamed *Noga* in 1980, and then *Alferdoss* in 1984. Renamed *American Star* in 1994, new owners wanted to use the 723ft-long liner as a hotel ship in Thailand. On 18 January 1994, while under tow and bound for Bangkok, the ship was wrecked off the Canary Islands and abandoned. She was later broken in two and sank.

PRESIDENT MONROE

Combination passenger–cargo ships, with a practical blend of revenue and purpose, became increasingly popular just before the start of the Second World War, but even more so in the late 1940s and 1950s. For its around-the-world service, San Francisco-based American President Lines built no less than six 96-passenger ships in 1940. The 1940-built *President Monroe* was one of this class.

QUEEN ELIZABETH

The world's largest liner at the time, the 83,673-ton *Queen Elizabeth* was due to begin commercial service in April 1940 to commemorate Cunard's centenary. But that was not to be – instead, for her safety in the face of war, she secretly fled to America months before, in February, and was then used as a troop transport throughout the war. She had to wait over six years, until October 1946, for a maiden trip to New York as a luxury liner.

The 2,283-passenger *Queen Elizabeth* served on the North Atlantic until 1968. Sold that same year to become a floating hotel–museum–convention centre at Port Everglades, Florida, the project failed. Sold again, in 1970, to C.Y. Tung, a Taiwanese shipping tycoon, she was to be made over as the *Seawise University*, the world's largest floating university–cruise ship. On the eve of her maiden voyage, however, on 9 January 1972, she burned and then capsized in Hong Kong harbour. Her remains were later scrapped on the spot.

Above: Sailing day: the *President Monroe* is off on another 95-day voyage around the world. (ALF Collection)

Below left: The *Queen Elizabeth* on sailing day from Southampton's Ocean Terminal. (Mick Lindsay Collection)

Below right: Overnight pause: the mighty *Queen Elizabeth* at New York's Pier 90. (Tim Noble Collection)

Morning arrival: the *Queen Elizabeth* approaches her Manhattan berth. (ALF Collection)

The towering *Queen Elizabeth* at Pier 90 (ALF Collection)

Paint job: the *Queen Elizabeth* at Hong Kong, being made over as the *Seawise University*. (ALF Collection)

BALTIKA

This 8,948grt ship might best be remembered for carrying Soviet premier Nikita Khruschev to New York in September 1960. She was, when completed by Dutch shipbuilders in 1940, the USSR's largest passenger ship, and was initially named *Vyacheslav Molotov*. She survived the war and went on to serve on the North Sea–Baltic run, between London and Leningrad. Renamed *Baltika* in 1957, the 444ft-long ship endured until 1986, when she was sold to be scrapped in Pakistan.

Left: Two queens: the *Queen Elizabeth* (left) and *Queen Mary* together at Pier 90 in a view from December 1948. (ALF Collection)

Below: The *Baltika* outbound at London. (Mick Lindsay Collection)

PRESIDENT ROOSEVELT

Fewer passenger ships have had more names. Built in 1944 as the troopship USS *General W P Richardson*, this 622ft-long ship was converted, during 1948–49, to a commercial passenger ship. She then sailed for a succession of owners as the *La Guardia, Leilani, President Roosevelt, Atlantis, Emerald Seas, Fantastica, Funtastica, Terrifica, Sun Fiesta, Sapphire Seas* and *Ocean Explorer*. She endured for sixty years, until scrapped in 2004.

WESTERDAM

This Holland–America 'combo ship' was sunk three times during the Second World War, but then salvaged, repaired and eventually used on the Rotterdam–New York passenger service. Entering service in 1946, this 12,149-ton ship carried up to 134 all first-class passengers.

Above: During a summertime cruise to Alaska, the largely rebuilt *President Roosevelt* calls at Vancouver. (ALF Collection)

Below: The *Westerdam* is the centre at the bottom in this 1963 aerial view of New York's Pier 40 – the *Statendam* is in the outer berth on the left, the *Rotterdam* at the top and the freighter *Kinderdyk* on the lower far right. (ALF Collection)

DEL NORTE

These three sisters were very fine examples of American combo-ship design – blending high-standard passenger quarters with lucrative cargo space. Used on the New Orleans–South America run, the *Del Mar*, *Del Norte* and *Del Sud* offered superb accommodation for 120 all first-class passengers.

PRESIDENT CLEVELAND

To revive the US–Far East, trans-Pacific passenger service just after the Second World War, the American President Lines took two intended troopships and had them redesigned and completed as passenger liners. The 1947–48 built *President Cleveland* and *President Wilson* were smart-looking passenger liners that carried up to 778 passengers in two classes.

STOCKHOLM

Notably, she was the very first newly built, transatlantic passenger ship to be commissioned following the Second World War. And she was noted as the largest passenger vessel built to date in Sweden.

Completed in the winter of 1948, this 11,700-ton combo liner was used on the Gothenburg–New York run. She is perhaps best remembered as the ship which collided with and sank Italy's *Andrea Doria* on 25–26 July 1956. The *Stockholm* went on to reach its seventieth year in 2018, having also been the *Volkerfreundschaft*, *Volker*, *Fridtjof Nansen*, *Italia I*, *Italia Prima*, *Valtur Prima*, *Caribe*, *Athena*, *Azores* and *Astoria*.

Above right: The former *Stockholm*, appearing here as the temporarily renamed *Volker* and awaiting sale at Southampton. (Author's Collection)

Below right: Badly damaged: The crushed bow of the *Stockholm* on 27 July 1956, following its collision with the *Andrea Doria*. The funnels of the *Queen of Bermuda* can be seen in the background. (ALF Collection)

Rebuilt almost beyond recognition, the former
Stockholm seen at Reykjavik, Iceland in June 2016 in
her new identity as the Portuguese-owned *Azores*.
(Author's Collection)

WILLEM RUYS

Still under construction when the Nazi armies invaded Holland in May 1940, this ship was to be Rotterdam Lloyd's largest and finest liner on the colonial run out to the Dutch East Indies. She was not completed until long after the war had ended, in November 1947. At 21,119 tons, she was used on the Rotterdam–Indonesia and later around-the-world runs, but was sold in 1964 to the Lauro Line (Italian flag) and rebuilt as the *Achille Lauro* (q.v.).

Sailing day: Holland's *Willem Ruys* departs from Wellington. (ALF Collection)

The *Media* is berthed at Pier 92 while the *Queen Elizabeth* arrives at the adjacent Pier 90. (ALF Collection)

The *Arosa Sky* was repainted in all-white for increased use as a cruise ship. (ALF Collection)

The beautiful *Caronia* in the Ocean Dock at Southampton – with the *Andes* on the left. (Mick Lindsay Collection)

MEDIA

Unusually for Cunard, this 13,345-ton passenger–cargo ship and its sister *Parthia* carried only 250 all first-class passengers. Completed in 1947–48, they were used on the Liverpool–New York run, but were largely unsuccessful. The *Media* was sold to the Italians in 1961 and rebuilt as the 1,224-berth *Flavia*; the *Parthia* changed hands to become the *Remuera* and then *Aramac*.

LA MARSEILLAISE / AROSA SKY

Another liner delayed by the Second World War was the *Marechal Petain* – soon renamed *La Marseillaise* – built in 1939–40 for France's Messageries Maritimes. She was to be the new, luxurious flagship for that company's colonial service between Marseilles and French Indo-China, but her construction was delayed, and the launch was postponed until 1944. The hull was then sunk by the retreating Germans. She was salvaged in 1946 and construction was resumed. The 17,321grt ship was finally completed in the summer of 1949 after almost a ten-year delay. Her French career was quite short, however. Sold and renamed *Arosa Sky* in 1957, she was sold again a year later, becoming the *Bianca C* for Italy's Costa Line. Her end came on 22 October 1961 when the 594ft-long liner caught fire off Grenada in the Caribbean, burned out and then sank two days later.

CARONIA

She was rated by many as the 'most luxurious' liner afloat in the 1950s. Large and very luxurious and likened to a 'big yacht', Cunard designed her for long cruises: around the world, around the Mediterranean and summers in Scandinavia. She had 600 handpicked staff and crew to look after the same number of passengers, but usually carried as few as a clubby 300 guests.

EDINBURGH CASTLE

To strengthen and revive its UK–South Africa service, the Union–Castle Line added its two largest liners yet, in 1948. The 28,705-ton *Edinburgh Castle* and her sister, the *Pretoria Castle*, became instant favourites. They could make the run between Southampton and Cape Town in thirteen days – as part of an extended itinerary including Southampton, Madeira or Las Palmas, Cape Town, Port Elizabeth, East London and Durban.

Lavender hull colouring: the *Edinburgh Castle* was one of the Union–Castle Line's largest liners. She is seen at Southampton. (Mick Lindsay Collection)

The *S A Oranje*, the former *Pretoria Castle*, on her final visit to Cape Town in 1975. She is en route to the breakers in Taiwan. (ALF Collection)

KARANJA

Some passenger ships never saw home waters. They traded elsewhere. The British India Steam Navigation Company's sister ships *Karanja* and *Kampala* were purposely created for Indian Ocean service, between South and East Africa and India. Although built in Scotland, they never returned to UK waters.

ORCADES

The Orient Line had lost a number of passenger ships during the Second World War and almost immediately, in 1945, began to plan for replacements. The company looked to bigger, well-decorated and quite fast ships, especially for the busy UK–Australia trade. The 28,164-ton, 1,545-passenger *Orcades* was the first, completed in 1948.

Above: Built for the India–Africa run, the *Karanja* and its sister *Kampala* were very popular ships. (Mick Lindsay Collection)

Below: Off on a cruise, the *Orcades* departs from Southampton. (Mick Lindsay Collection)

HIMALAYA

P&O also lost some of their passenger liners during the war – and so they too set about rebuilding in the late 1940s. The 27,955grt *Himalaya* was the first, completed in 1949. Generally, she was routed from London to Gibraltar, Suez, Aden, Bombay, Colombo, Fremantle, Melbourne and Sydney.

ÎLE DE FRANCE (POST-WAR)

Some liners underwent extensive refurbishing, even rebuilding and modernisation following the Second World War. Post-war refits seemed the ideal time for long stays in shipyards. The celebrated *Île de France* was given a new, more contemporary look – her original three funnels came off and were replaced by two of a more modern design.

Above left: On her farewell visit, the *Himalaya* is seen in Melbourne in 1974. (Tim Noble Collection)

Below left: Late-morning departure for the *Île de France* – the *Liberté* is on the left; the *United States* on the right. (ALF Collection)

Opposite: Rebuilt after the Second World War with two funnels, the modernised *Île de France* carefully docks herself at New York's Pier 88 during a tugboat strike. (ALF Collection)

The handsome-looking *Oslofjord* berthed at Southampton during its 1967 charter to the Greek Line. (Mick Lindsay Collection)

OSLOFJORD

The pre-war *Oslofjord* of the Norwegian America Line was a handsome ship, but a tragic one. She was sunk in December 1940 when only two years old. Consequently, the owners set about building a replacement: a new *Oslofjord*, Dutch-built and ready in 1949 for North Atlantic service between Oslo, Bergen, Copenhagen and New York. Later chartered to the Greek Line (1967–68) and then the Costa Line (1968–70), she was renamed *Fulvia* in her final days before burning and then sinking off the Canary Islands on 20 July 1970.

Lots of ships: the *Rangitane* seen in London's Royal Albert Dock in a view dated June 1966. (Mick Lindsay Collection)

RANGITANE

The 21,867grt *Rangitane* and *Rangitoto* were among the very largest combination passenger–cargo liners ever built. Carrying up to 416 passengers and provided with six cargo holds, they were built in 1948–49 for Britain's New Zealand Shipping Co. They were used on the long haul run between London, Auckland and Wellington – via Curacao, the Panama Canal and Tahiti.

LIBERTÉ

When US–Allied forces entered the port of Bremerhaven in May 1945, they found the rusting *Europa*, then the third-largest liner afloat. She was soon revived by the Americans and used to ferry troops homeward to New York. But there were many problems, including lots of on-board fires, and the 936ft-long ship was soon deemed inadequate and troublesome. United States Lines considered rebuilding her as their flagship, but instead she was given to the French as reparations, namely for the loss of the *Normandie* four years before. Thoroughly rebuilt and upgraded over three years, she resumed sailing in August 1950 as the *Liberté*, the 'new' flagship of the French Line.

Left: Winter morning: the *Liberté* at New York's Pier 88. (Author's Collection)

Below: Manhattan afternoon: the *Liberté* is across from Cunard's *Caronia*. The 77-story Chrysler Building is in centre position. (Author's Collection)

Completely rebuilt, the migrant ship *New Australia* at Southampton.
(Norman Knebel Collection)

NEW AUSTRALIA/ARKADIA

One of the more extensive rebuilds after the war was that of Furness–Bermuda Line's *Monarch of Bermuda*. While refitting to resume New York–Bermuda service, she caught fire and was declared a complete loss. A second appraisal, however, saw her hull, machinery and some upper decks saved. Having had three funnels, she was rebuilt with a single stack and also a unique smoke-dispensing bipod mast as the migrant ship *New Australia*. Mostly, she sailed on the UK–Australia run. In 1958, the 580ft-long ship was sold to the Greek Line and became their *Arkadia*.

CHUSAN

To greatly strengthen its London–Far East service, P&O Lines added the 24,215grt *Chusan* in 1950. Carrying up to 1,026 passengers in two classes, she sailed out from London via Suez, Bombay, Colombo, Singapore, Hong Kong, Kobe and Yokohama.

AUREOL

Colonial passenger ship services were revived after the war and these included the UK–West Africa trade for Britain's Elder Dempster Lines. That Liverpool-based company added its biggest and finest passenger ship, the 14,083grt, 353-passenger *Aureol*, in 1951.

AUGUSTUS

Italy's liner fleet was much depleted after the war and so massive rebuilding became the order of the day. The Italian Line opted to build its first pair of big liners in 1951–52 for the South Atlantic rather than the North and these were the handsome sister ships *Giulio Cesare* and *Augustus*. These 27,078-ton ships could carry up to 1,180 passengers – 178 in first class, 288 in cabin class and 714 in tourist class. They were run between Naples and Genoa and then across the South Atlantic to Rio, Santos, Montevideo and Buenos Aires.

Above left: Southern waters: P&O's *Chusan* calls at Cape Town. (Mick Lindsay Collection)

Below left: Moody reflection: the *Aureol* at dock in Liverpool. (Author's Collection)

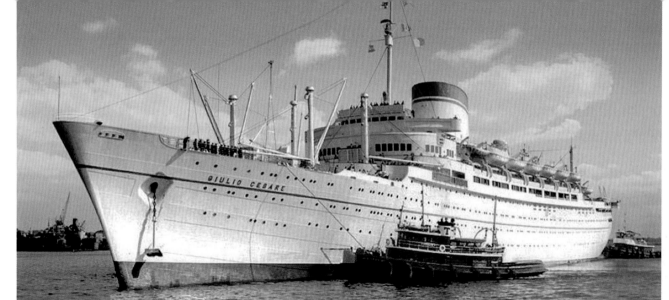

The *Giulio Cesare* arrives in Boston for a short call as part of a New York–Mediterranean voyage. (ALF Collection)

Stern-first: the *Augustus* berthed at Naples between voyages to South America. (ALF Collection)

INDEPENDENCE/CONSTITUTION

With Italian liners slowly reappearing after the Second World War, America wanted its share of the New York–Mediterranean trade. American Export Lines added the superb, 29,500-ton sisters *Independence* and *Constitution* in 1951. While also intended as big troopships should another war arise, they were noteworthy as being the first fully air-conditioned big liners. Withdrawn from transatlantic service in the late 1960s, they finished their days as highly popular Hawaiian cruise ships.

Above left: Being refuelled, the *Constitution* seen on the south side of Pier 84, New York. The huge gas tank behind was pulled down in 1968. (ALF Collection)

Below left: The *Constitution* arriving at New York in this 1964 view. Behind are the *United States*, *Berlin*, *Queen Elizabeth*, *Homeric* and *Empress of Canada*. (Author's Collection)

AUSTRALIA/DONIZETTI

Lloyd Triestino build three passenger ships, in 1951, for its Italy–Australia trade. Carrying up to 792 passengers in three classes, these ships, named *Australia*, *Neptunia* and *Oceania*, were quite handsome, very contemporary-looking liners. Uniquely, they were capped by low, domed funnels. Transferred to the Italian Line in 1963 for its Italy–west coast of South America service, the three ships were renamed *Donizetti*, *Verdi* and *Rossini* respectively.

Above: Restyled as the Italian Line's *Donizetti*, the former *Australia* of Lloyd Triestino is seen at Naples. (Mick Lindsay Collection)]

Below: Saturday afternoon: the *Ocean Monarch* at Pier 95, New York – with the *Queen of Bermuda* just behind. This photo dates from 1964. (Author's Collection)

OCEAN MONARCH

To join the larger, very popular *Queen of Bermuda* on the weekly New York–Bermuda trade, the Furness–Bermuda Line built a smaller ship, which could also cruise on longer itineraries. Carrying 440 all first-class passengers, the 13,654grt *Ocean Monarch* was introduced in the spring of 1951 and proved very successful from the start. Among other amenities, she offered private bathroom facilities in every cabin.

ORONSAY

Orient Line's next new build for their Australian liner service was the 27,632-ton *Oronsay*, completed in 1951 and slightly larger than the earlier, similar-looking *Orcades* of 1948. Used as well on the UK–Australia trade, the *Oronsay* could carry up to 1,416 passengers in two classes.

Above: Fond farewell: the *Oronsay* departs from Southampton for the last time. (Mick Lindsay Collection)

Left: Quiet afternoon: the funnel of the *Oronsay*. (Author's Collection)

Port of call: the *Rhodesia Castle* at Mombasa, during one of her round-Africa voyages. (Author's Collection)

RHODESIA CASTLE

In addition to their famed express service to the South African Cape, the Union–Castle Line also ran a passenger service that went completely around continental Africa. The long voyage lasted sixty-four days and was routed east-about: the following voyage was west-about with the ports in reverse. For these itineraries, the company added three new liners in 1951–52: the *Braemar Castle*, *Kenya Castle* and *Rhodesia Castle*.

RYNDAM

With great foresight, the Holland–America Line saw a bright future in economy travel on the North Atlantic. And so, in 1951–52, the Company added the 15,015grt *Ryndam* and her sister, the *Maasdam*, which were purposely designed to carry thirsty-six passengers in first class and 836 in tourist class. They also offered great economy: $20 per person per day in the 1950s. Used on the North Atlantic, they were also popular, off-season cruise ships.

Noontime departure: The *Ryndam* departing from New York's Pier 40. (ALF Collection)

Maiden call: the *Andrea Doria* calling at Gibraltar for the first time, in January 1953. (Mick Lindsay Collection)

ANDREA DORIA

An important ship in her own right, but made far more famous because of her tragic loss: the liner of Italy's post-war 'maritime renaissance' became her 'ship of tragedy'. Completed in December 1952, the 29,083-ton *Andrea Doria* had a short career. Rammed by the Swedish liner *Stockholm* while off Nantucket on 25 July 1956, the 700ft-long Italian flagship sank the next day. Fifty-two people perished.

MAASDAM

A very popular Holland–America liner, this 503ft-long ship, completed in the summer of 1952, had two, long careers: first for the Dutch, and then for the Poles as the *Stefan Batory* (q.v.).

UGANDA

This 1952-built ship also had two careers – first as a two-class passenger–cargo ship on the London–East Africa for the British India Steam Navigation Co. Ltd; then, beginning in 1968, as an educational cruise ship for an affiliate, BI Cruises.

UNITED STATES

Unquestionably, she was one of the most outstanding liners of all time: the pride of the American fleet and an extraordinary example of maritime engineering. Completed in the spring of 1952, it was reported that she reached an amazing 43 knots during her sea trials and also did 20 knots in reverse. Her maiden voyage that July, from New York to Southampton, was also a blazing success: a crossing of three days and ten hours at an average speed of 35.59 knots. Carrying up to 1,928 passengers in three classes, this 53,329-ton liner regularly sailed between New York, Le Havre and Southampton (and occasionally out to Bremerhaven). Retired in November 1969, she has been idle ever since – the subject of numerous revival plans and schemes, none of which has come to pass. She has been berthed in Philadelphia since 1996.

Above left: Farewell: the *Maasdam* departing from Bremerhaven in this 1964 scene. (Mick Lindsay Collection)

Centre left: Offloading and then reloading cargo: the *Uganda* lying in London Docks. (Mick Lindsay Collection)

Below left: Panorama of Manhattan's West Side: as seen from a skyscraper roof, five liners are in port in this 1958 view – (from left to right) *Cristoforo Colombo, America, United States. Queen Elizabeth* and *Stockholm.* (Author's Collection)

Wintery morning: Moran tugs carefully berth the *United States* into Pier 86 in an ice-filled Hudson River. (ALF Collection)

Right: Red, white and blue colouring: the huge funnels aboard the *United States*. (ALF Collection)

Right: Red, white and blue colouring: the huge funnels aboard the *United States*. (ALF Collection)

Below: Coming and going: the *United States* is soon to depart as the *Queen Mary* arrives. (ALF Collection)

Bottom: Aglow in lights: the *Cristoforo Colombo* at Pier 84, New York. (ALF Collection)

CRISTOFORO COLOMBO

A very fine ship in its own right, she is perhaps best known as the sister ship to the ill-fated *Andrea Doria*. Used on the Italy–New York run until 1973 and then on the Italy–South America service, this 29,191-ton ship became a hotel ship at Puerto Ordaz, Venezuela in 1977. Sold to Taiwanese scrappers in 1981, the demolition was postponed and she was idle at Hong Kong until finally scrapped (in Taiwan) in 1983.

KUNGSHOLM/EUROPA (1953)

A very lovely ship in several ways, this 600-footer went on to have three careers: Swedish, West German and Italian. Built in Holland and completed in late 1953, this handsome-looking, twin-funnel liner was completed as the *Kungsholm*, flagship of the Swedish–America Line. It was used on the Gothenburg–Copenhagen–New York run, and for cruising. Carrying 802 passengers in two classes, she was sold to the North German Lloyd line in 1965 and renamed *Europa*. Sold again in 1981 to the Costa Line, she became the *Columbus C*. Her days ended after she rammed a breakwater and sank at Cadiz, Spain on 29 July 1984. Later salvaged, she was scrapped in Spain in 1985.

EUROPA (1953)

In addition to its Italy–Australia liner service, Lloyd Triestino also ran passenger services to South and East Africa and to India and the Far East. Two sets of smart-looking sister ships were created for each service in the early 1950s. The *Asia* and *Victoria* handled the Eastern run; the *Africa* and *Europa* worked the African trades. The 11,430-ton *Europa* could carry up to 484 passengers in three classes.

Opposite above left: Strung with lights and soon off on a cruise, the Swedish *Kungsholm* is seen at Pier 97. (ALF Collection)

Opposite above right: Restyled as the German *Europa*, the same ship is docked at Pier 88 on its maiden call under its second name in January 1966. The stern of the *United States* can be seen on the right. (Author's Collection)

Opposite below: Italian streamline: Lloyd Triestino's *Europa* arriving at Cape Town. (Mick Lindsay Collection)

OLYMPIA

She was supposed to be the pride of the Greek merchant marine, but at her launch, in April 1953, there was a dispute. The owners, the Greek Line, abruptly changed the new, 23,000-ton liner's registry to a flag of convenience: Liberia. Used mostly on the Mediterranean–New York run, this 1,307-berth liner was retired and laid-up from 1974–82. Afterwards, having been sold to Commodore Cruise Lines, she was rebuilt as the *Caribe I* for Miami–Caribbean cruising. Sold again in 1993, to Regal Cruises, she changed to *Regal Empress*. After fifty-six years, she was scrapped in 2009.

SANTA MARIA

The Belgian-built *Santa Maria* and her sister *Vera Cruz* were Portugal's biggest and finest liners when completed in 1952–53. Carrying some 1,078 passengers divided in three classes, these ships were designed for Latin American services from Lisbon. While the *Vera Cruz* tended to serve Brazil, the 609ft-long *Santa Maria* was routed on a more mid Atlantic run: to the Caribbean and to Port Everglades, Florida.

ARCADIA

The 723ft-long *Arcadia* and her near-sister *Iberia* were P&O's biggest liners by the mid 1950s and they were sensations on the UK–Australia run. They were big, powerful and well decorated. However, while the 29,734-ton, Clydebank-built *Arcadia* went on to a long, very successful and popular career, the Belfast-built *Iberia* was troubled, plagued with engine and operational problems for most of her days.

Above left: Greek flagship: the *Olympia* is seen off Dover in this 1953 view. (Author's Collection)

Below left: Tropical waters: the Portuguese *Santa Maria* at Curacao in 1961. (ALF Collection)

Cruising to Alaska: the *Arcadia* seen in Glacier Bay in 1969. (ALF Collection)

Fond farewell: the *Iberia* on her final call to Melbourne in February 1972. (Frank Andrews Collection)

Above: With her modern domed funnel, the *Saxonia* on trials in 1954. (Author's Collection)

Below: New look: the *Saxonia* and *Ivernia* were extensively refitted at the John Brown shipyard at Clydebank as the green-painted *Carmania* and *Franconia*. (Mick Lindsay Collection)

IBERIA

While a fine-looking ship, the *Iberia* was, as mentioned above, not a good operational ship. One crewmember said, 'It was as if she was cursed – even crew members avoided the *Iberia*! She had mechanical problems, small fires, fuel leaks and even stability problems. And once, even the funnel caught on fire.' At only eighteen years of age, the 1,406-passenger *Iberia* was sold for scrap.

SAXONIA/CARMANIA

Cunard's very last traditional Atlantic passenger liners were a quartet of 23,000 tonners for the seasonal UK–Canada run. Each carried some 900 passengers and considerable cargo, but unfortunately they were not intended for profit-making wintertime cruising. The 608ft-long *Saxonia*, launched in February 1954 and commissioned into commercial service the following September, was the first of this foursome. She was assigned to the London–Le Havre–Quebec City–Montreal route between April and December; for the remainder of the year, she sailed to Halifax and New York.

IVERNIA/FRANCONIA

Within less than a decade of completing their traditional passenger liners in the early 1950s, Cunard realised that cruising was an inevitable and undeniable alternative to the established form of transatlantic service. So, two of the ships, the *Saxonia* and *Ivernia*, were sent back to their builders, John Brown's yard on the Clyde, and, in 1962–63, were extensively refitted. New public rooms, a lido deck with a pool and exterior green colouring were added. The ships also received new names – the *Saxonia* changed to *Carmania*, and the *Ivernia* became *Franconia*.

In 1973, both ships were sold to the Soviets, becoming the *Leonid Sobinov* and *Feodor Shalyapin*.

ORSOVA

Built in the wake of the highly successful *Orcades* (1948) and *Oronsay* (1951), the 28,790-ton *Orsova* of 1954 was similar, but with one noted difference: she did not have a traditional mast. Instead, rigging was attached between king posts and the ship's very dominant single funnel.

Above: Three-day visit: the *Franconia* berthed at Hamilton, Bermuda – with Moore–McCormack Lines' *Argentina* just behind. (Mick Lindsay Collection)

Right: With her corn-coloured hull, the *Orsova* is seen at San Francisco. (Mick Lindsay Collection)

Innovative: the engines-aft *Southern Cross* carried only passengers and no cargo. (Mick Lindsay Collection)

SOUTHERN CROSS

In some ways, the Shaw Savill Line's *Southern Cross* was one of the most significant liners of the 1950s. Built at Belfast and completed in the winter of 1955, this 20,000grt ship was innovative: she carried only one class of passengers, but in greater comfort; her engines and therefore her funnel were both placed aft offering more open deck space for the cruising travellers; and she was a pure passenger ship – no cargo was carried whatsoever.

BERGENSFJORD

She was the national flagship, and Norway's largest liner to date. She did Atlantic crossings for half the year, and cruising for the other half: an increasingly common combination. She went on, beginning in 1971, to become the French Line's *De Grasse*, and after that the Far East-based cruise ship *Rasa Sayang*.

World cruising: the *Bergensfjord* passes through the Panama Canal toward the end of her 99-day cruise around the world. (Mick Lindsay Collection)

BAUDOUINVILLE/CATHAY

Combination passenger–cargo liners were still suitable for some services such as Belgium to the colonial Congo and from the UK to the distant Far East. The 301-passenger, all-one-class *Baudouinville* was completed for the Belgians in 1957, but then sold to P&O some three years later, becoming the *Cathay*. Her sister ship, the *Jadotville*, followed suit and later became P&O's *Chitral*.

MARIPOSA

Some ship owners opted to take existing hulls (with existing propulsion machinery) and convert these to passenger liners. Two big, fast Mariner Class freighters, built in 1952–53, were sold to the Matson Line three years later and rebuilt as luxury passenger liners: the 365-bed sisters *Mariposa* and *Monterey*. Both proved very successful on the six-week round trip run from San Francisco to the South Pacific, Australia and New Zealand.

NEVASA

She and a similar ship, the *Oxfordshire* of the Bibby Line, were the very last peacetime troopships built by the British Government. The 20,527grt *Nevasa* of the British India Line was commissioned in 1956 and carried 1,500 passengers divided in four classes. She was, however, refitted as an educational 'schools' cruise ship in 1964.

Above right: Far Eastern sailings: the sister ships *Cathay* and *Chitral* had very handsome exteriors. (Mick Lindsay Collection)

Centre right: Pier 35, San Francisco: the *Mariposa* is on the left; the *Lurline* on the right. (ALF Collection)

Below right: Already stripped of most of her lifeboats, the *Nevasa* is seen on her final voyage, from Malta to the breakers in Taiwan in 1975. (Mick Lindsay Collection)

Off on a cruise, the *Reina Del Mar* is seen departing from Southampton. (Mick Lindsay Collection)

The good-looking *Ausonia*, flagship of Italy's Adriatica Line. (Mick Lindsay Collection)

REINA DEL MAR

The Pacific Steam Navigation Company's smart-looking *Reina Del Mar* was created in the final years of the Liverpool–west coast of South America service, when the route was barely profitable. Completed in 1956, her useful days in that trade came to an end, however, within seven years – in 1963. Quickly, she was made over as a cruise ship, but sailing under the house flag of the Union–Castle Line.

EMPRESS OF ENGLAND

Designed for the seasonal Liverpool–Montreal run, the *Empress of England* and her sister ship, the *Empress of Britain*, spent the winter, off-season on cruises, usually from New York to the sunny waters of the Caribbean. Carrying up to 1,058 passengers, the accommodation was divided between two classes – 160 first class and 898 tourist class.

AUSONIA

'In the 1950s, she was the queen of the Mediterranean – the finest liner sailing within the confines of those sunny waters,' noted the late Frank Braynard. Built in 1957 and based partly on designs from the earlier *Andrea Doria*, the 11,879-ton *Ausonia* was the flagship of Italy's Adriatica Line and used on their express run from Italy to Lebanon and Egypt. At 522 feet in length, this handsome-looking liner could carry 185 first-class passengers and a further 135 in second class and 252 in third class.

CABO SAN ROQUE

The *Cabo San Roque* and its sister *Cabo San Vicente* were Spain's largest and most luxurious liners when completed in the late 1950s. Spanish-built, designed and decorated, these 14,491-ton ships were created especially for the Mediterranean–east coast of South America services of the Ybarra Line.

Summer cruising: Spain's *Cabo San Roque* is anchored in Norway's Geirangerfjord. (ALF Collection)

GRIPSHOLM (1957)

She was appraised as one of the finest liners of the 1950s. Built by the Ansaldo Shipyard at Genoa, the 23,100-ton *Gripsholm* had the classic lines of twin funnels and twin masts; inside, her interiors were described as warm, inviting and luxurious. She spent the summers on the Gothenburg–New York run; the remainder of the year, she went cruising – mostly on long, luxurious itineraries.

STATENDAM (1957)

The earlier, but smaller *Ryndam* and *Maasdam* (q.v.) had been successful catering largely to the tourist class market: their example led to the larger, more comfortable *Statendam*. Completed in 1957, this 642ft-long liner could carry 952 passengers – 84 in first class and 868 in tourist. She was designed to spend two-thirds of the year on the transatlantic run between Rotterdam and New York; the remainder as a cruise ship.

Above: Another summer cruise: the *Gripsholm* is in Norwegian waters during a 45-day North Cape–Scandinavia sailing. (Des Kirkpatrick Collection)

Below: Handsome lines: the fine-looking *Statendam*, commissioned in 1957. (ALF Collection)

SANTA ROSA (1958)

America added four new liners in 1958: the sisters *Santa Rosa* and *Santa Paula* for the Grace Line; then the sisters *Brasil* and *Argentina* for the Moore–McCormack Lines. The 15,371-ton *Santa Rosa* and her sister, carrying up to 300 all first-class passengers, were designed for New York–Caribbean service. Their design was based upon the earlier *United States*.

ARGENTINA

The 553-passenger *Argentina* and *Brasil* were created for a longer service: New York to the east coast of South America. Rebuilt slightly in 1963, their lives under the Moore–McCormack Lines and the US flag were quite short, however. Laid-up in 1969, they were sold two years later to the Holland–America Line and rebuilt as dedicated cruise ships. The *Argentina* went on to become the *Veendam* and later the *Brasil*, *Monarch Star*, *Bermuda Star*, *Enchanted Isle*, *Commodore Hotel*, before reverting to *Enchanted Isle*.

ATLANTIC

The 900-passenger *Atlantic* was another conversion: built in 1953 as a freighter, she was rebuilt in 1958 to become a passenger liner. First used by American Banner Lines on their New York–Amsterdam service, she joined American Export Lines for New York–Mediterranean sailings in 1960. Laid-up in 1967, this 564ft-long liner later became an educational cruise ship, a 'floating university'.

Above right: Maiden arrival: the Grace Line's *Santa Rosa* arrives in New York harbour for the first time in June 1958. (Author's Collection)

Centre right: Norwegian waters: the *Argentina* seen during her summertime Northlands Cruise. (Des Kirkpatrick Collection)

Below right: A former freighter, the *Atlantic* of American Export Lines is berthed at Pier 84, New York. (Author's Collection)

HANSEATIC

When Canadian Pacific retired their 27-year-old *Empress of Scotland* in 1957, she might have gone to the breakers but instead found buyers in the form of West Germany's Hamburg–Atlantic Line. Sent to a Hamburg shipyard, she was extensively rebuilt and modernised. The original three funnels came off and were replaced by two more contemporary ones. The 'new' *Hanseatic* entered North Atlantic service between Hamburg and New York in the summer of 1958.

PENDENNIS CASTLE

By the mid 1950s, the Union–Castle Line began thinking of replacing some of their older liners. Three new liners were soon on the drawing boards. The 28,582-ton, 763ft-long *Pendennis Castle* came first, in late 1958. Used on the express service between Southampton, Cape Town and Durban, she could carry up to 736 passengers and a considerable amount of cargo.

BREMEN (1959)

In 1958–59, the North German Lloyd line also converted an existing liner – the French *Pasteur* (built 1939) – and thoroughly rebuilt it as the 'new' *Bremen*. Looking more contemporary, the 697ft-long liner carrying up to 1,200 passengers in two classes was used on the Bremerhaven–New York run for most of the year and for cruising in the remainder.

Above left: Rebuilt from the three-funnel *Empress of Scotland*, the same ship reappeared in 1958 as the twin-funnel *Hanseatic*. (Mick Lindsay Collection)

Below left: Summer crossing: having sailed from Cuxhaven, Southampton and Cherbourg, the *Hanseatic* heads for New York. (ALF Collection)

ROTTERDAM

By the late 1950s, new national flagships were in the works for several major transatlantic companies. The Dutch planned for the *Rotterdam* (1959), the Italians had the *Leonardo da Vinci* (1960) and, biggest of all, the French had their *France* (1962).

The 38,645grt *Rotterdam*, introduced in September 1959, was a Dutch tour de force – a most beautiful ship in every way. She was also the first Atlantic liner to dispense with the traditional funnel and instead use uptakes placed aft. This 748ft liner remains afloat, serving as a museum, hotel and convention centre in Rotterdam harbour.

ARLANZA

In what proved to be the twilight years of their long-established UK–east coast of South America service, the Royal Mail Lines added three combination passenger–cargo liners: *Amazon*, *Aragon* and *Arlanza*. These 20,350-ton combo liners (carrying up to 464 passengers in three classes) were in fact the last British liners to have three classes and the last to carry third-class passengers. Retired after little more than a decade of service, each ship was later converted to a car carrier.

Above: Innovation: with no traditional funnel, the superb *Rotterdam* in home port waters. (ALF Collection)

Below: The Royal Mail Lines' three-class *Arlanza* at London – with the Blue Star Line's *Argentina Star* to the far left. (Mick Lindsay Collection)

VICTORIA (1936)

The work of designers and shipyards can be quite remarkable. An older, rather ordinary passenger ship (the *Dunnottar Castle*, built in 1936) can be converted, even transformed (in 1958–59) into a modern cruise ship. The *Victoria* of the Incres Line was re-designed as a full-time cruise liner, carrying 600 passengers in luxurious, all first-class quarters, and with amenities such as complete air conditioning, a two-deck high theatre, private bathroom facilities in every cabin and a vast lido deck with twin swimming pools.

LEONARDO DA VINCI

When commissioned in the spring of 1960, Italian Line confidently predicted that their new, 33,300-ton flagship *Leonardo da Vinci* would most likely be converted to nuclear propulsion within five years, by 1965. This never to came to pass, but the 1,326-passenger ship was a great success and very popular on the New York–Mediterranean run. Converted to a full-time cruise ship in her later years, she burned out and then capsized while laid-up in July 1980. Her remains were demolished two years later.

Above left: Rebuilt from the *Dunnottar Castle*, the vastly rebuilt cruise ship *Victoria* later had her name restyled slightly as *The Victoria*. (Mick Lindsay Collection)

Below left: Off on a Caribbean cruise: late-night sailing for the *Leonardo da Vinci*. (Author's Collection)

ORIANA

She proved to be the last of the famed Orient Line passenger liners before, in 1960, the company was incorporated into the merged company P&O–Orient Lines. She was also the largest Orient liner ever – and the fastest. The 41,900-ton *Oriana* cut the passage time from Southampton to Sydney via Suez from four to three weeks. Used in UK–Australia and around-the-world service, the 2,134-bed ship later became a full-time cruise ship before being sold to Japanese and Chinese buyers for use as a museum–floating hotel–entertainment centre. During a typhoon, she capsized at Dalian in 2004 and was salvaged a year later only to be scrapped.

Fastest to Sydney: the innovative and speedy *Oriana*, departing from Sydney. (Mick Lindsay Collection)

Farewell to Cape Town: the *Windsor Castle* on her last commercial voyage to Southampton in September 1977. (ALF Collection)

WINDSOR CASTLE

Ceremoniously named by HM Queen Elizabeth the Queen Mother at the Cammell Laird Shipyard just across from Liverpool in June 1959, the 37,640-ton *Windsor Castle* was the largest Union–Castle liner of all. Commissioned into service in the summer of 1960, the 822-passenger ship was used on the UK–South Africa express run until 1977 and then, after being sold to Greek buyers, was used as an accommodation ship in Saudi Arabia. She had made 124 round voyages to Africa and carried 270,000 passengers. Laid-up in Greece from 1992, the 783ft-long liner was sold for scrap in India in 2005.

CANBERRA

Together with the *Oriana*, the 45,733grt, 818ft-long *Canberra* was, to many, the greatest liner ever built for the UK–Australia trade. In a class of her own, the 2,272-passenger *Canberra* was quite extraordinary – fast, sleek and with modern décor. Built at Belfast and completed in 1961, she was used primarily for cruising after 1973, until her retirement in 1997. Sold for scrapping in Pakistan in October 1997, she took a year to demolish.

FUNCHAL

1961 was a notable year for Portuguese shipping – three new passenger liners were completed. The 9,800grt *Funchal* was the smallest, being created for Empresa Insulana's Lisbon–Madeira–Azores service. Carrying some 550 passengers in three classes, she was used in later years as a one-class cruise ship. Retired in 2016, she remains laid-up at Lisbon at the time of writing (2019).

INFANTE DOM HENRIQUE

Belgian-built, the 23,306grt *Infante Dom Henrique* was the new flagship of Lisbon-based Companhia Colonial. A sleek-looking vessel, she was designed for the West, South and East African service and could carry up to 1,018 passengers in two classes. Laid-up from 1976–88 at Sines, Portugal, a plan to convert the ship to a moored hotel never materialised. Instead, she was sold and refitted as a cruise ship in 1988 and was renamed *Vasco da Gama*. She began sailing for Seawind Cruise Lines (Panamanian flag) in 1991 and was marketed as the *Seawind Crown*, but never officially renamed. She was broken up in 2004.

The magnificent *Canberra*, the largest liner ever for the UK–Australia trade. (Mick Lindsay Collection)

Largest of the Portuguese–African liners, the *Infante Dom Henrique* is at Cape Town in this view. (Mick Lindsay Collection)

Above: During a transatlantic cruise in 1974, the *Principe Perfeito* is outbound at New York. (Mick Lindsay Collection)

Below: Farewell to South Africa: the *S A Vaal* makes her final sailing from Cape Town. (Author's Collection)

PRINCIPE PERFEITO

The third new Portuguese liner, the 19,393-ton *Principe Perfeito*, belonged to Companhia Nacional and was commissioned in 1961. She too served on the African run, between Lisbon and West, South and East African ports. She carried up to 1,200 passengers in three classes. Sold in 1976, she then became the accommodation ship *Al Hasa* operating in the Middle East before being sold to the Sitmar Line in 1980, who intended to rebuild her as the cruise ship *Fairsky*. This never happened, however, and the ship was renamed *Vera* and then *Marianna IX* for use as a Saudi Arabian hotel ship. Laid-up in Greece in 1992, the 625ft-long ship was finally sold to Indian scrappers in 2001.

TRANSVAAL CASTLE/S A VAAL

When completed in 1962, she was the last liner for the Union–Castle Line. Built on the Clyde, she introduced the idea of 'hotel class' – 728 passengers in one-class accommodation. She was renamed *S A Vaal* in 1966 and transferred to the Safmarine Lines under the South African flag in 1969. Sold to Carnival Cruise Lines in 1977, she was rebuilt in Japan as the 1,432-passenger cruise ship *Festivale* for Miami–Caribbean cruising. Sold again in 1996, she became the *Island Breeze* and later *Big Red Boat III*. Laid-up in 2000, she was sold to Indian ship-breakers in 2003.

Engines-aft design: the *Northern Star* departs from Southampton on another round-the-world voyage. (Mick Lindsay Collection)

NORTHERN STAR

The 1955-built *Southern Cross* had been so successful that a slightly larger version was ordered by the Shaw Savill Line. The 24,731-ton, 1,437-passenger *Northern Star* entered around-the-world service in 1962. Not an especially successful ship (she was plagued with mechanical problems), she sailed for little more than twelve years. She was demolished in Taiwan in 1974–75.

FRANCE/NORWAY

The last of the great French liners, the 1,035ft *France* also ranked as the longest liner afloat. Laid down in 1957 and launched in May 1960, she entered Le Havre–New York service in February 1962. She carried up to 1,944 passengers – 501 in first class and 1,443 in tourist. The 66,348-ton liner had a shortened career, however – she was laid-up from 1974–79. Sold to Norwegian Caribbean Lines, she was rebuilt as the cruise ship *Norway* in 1979–80. She was further rebuilt in 1990, when her tonnage was relisted as 76,049 and her maximum capacity as 2,565.

Following a boiler explosion at Miami in May 2003, the ship was towed to Germany and laid-up until 2005. She was then towed to Port Klang, Malaysia and again laid-up. Plans to revive her never materialised and, in 2006, she was renamed *Blue Lady*. She was delivered to Indian scrappers in 2008.

Above: Winter rendezvous: the mighty *France* as seen from the *Leonardo da Vinci* at Curacao. Both ships were on Caribbean cruises. (Des Kirkpatrick Collection)

Below: The *France* is seen off Lower Manhattan, departing on an afternoon in March 1962. (Author's Collection)

Left: The *Norway* departing from New York on a transatlantic cruise in September 2001. (Author's Collection)

Below: The rebuilt, modernised *Irpinia* originally dated from 1929. (Mick Lindsay Collection)

IRPINIA

Older liners were given refits and facelifts in the 1960s. The 1929-built *Irpinia*, owned by Italy's Grimaldi–Siosa Lines, was modernised in 1962. Uniquely, her tapered single funnel gives the 537ft-long ship a far more modern appearance in defiance of her actual age. She had been the French *Campana* until 1955 and then, after being bought by the Italians, began a series of refits that increased her capacity to over 1,200. Used mostly on the Europe–West Indies run, she spent her later years as a cruise ship. Finally scrapped in 1983, she was by then fifty-four years old.

QUEEN OF BERMUDA (REFITTED)

The veteran *Queen of Bermuda* also had 'surgery', in 1961–62, changing from three funnels to one. It gave the then 29-year-old liner a far more modern look. The ship endured for just under four more years before going to the breakers in late 1966.

LAKONIA

Another veteran, Greek Line's *Lakonia*, finished her days as a contemporary cruise ship. She had been Holland's *Johan van Oldenbarnevelt*, dating from 1930 and created then for the colonial service between Amsterdam and the Dutch East Indies. The Dutch had modernised her in 1959 and, following the purchase by the Greeks in 1962, she was used as a full-time cruise ship. Unfortunately, on her Christmas cruise in 1963, she caught fire off Madeira, burned out and later, when abandoned and empty, sank. There were 128 casualties.

Above: Final cruise: the *Queen of Bermuda* departs for Bermuda on her final cruise in November 1966. (Author's Collection)

Below: The former *Johan van Oldenbarnevelt* of 1930 became the Greek Line cruise ship *Lakonia* in 1962. (Mick Lindsay Collection)

FAIRSTAR

The 1957-built, British troopship *Oxfordshire* was thoroughly rebuilt in 1963–64 as the liner *Fairstar* for the Sitmar Line. Restyled from 1,500 passengers in four classes to 1,900 in all one class, she was thoroughly modernised and improved for Europe–Australia and around-the-world service. The 609ft-long liner became a full-time cruise ship in 1975, sailing only from Australia.

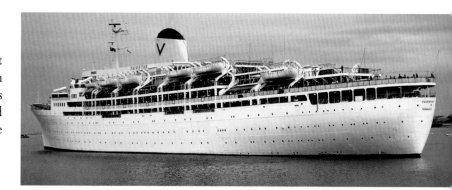

GALILEO GALILEI & GUGLIELMO MARCONI

Italy had a boom period in building new liners in the early 1960s and this cohort included the country's finest and fastest liners for the Australian trade. The twins *Galileo Galilei* and *Guglielmo Marconi* were completed in 1963 and each carried up to 1,750 passengers in two classes. Sleek, modern and powerful, they were related in design to the earlier *Leonardo da Vinci* and the subsequent *Michelangelo* and *Raffaello*.

ALEXANDR PUSHKIN

The Soviet Union used an East German shipyard to construct five 750-passenger sister ships between 1964 and 1972. They were named *Ivan Franko*, *Alexandr Pushkin*, *Taras Shevchenko*, *Shota Rustavelli* and *Mikhal Lermontov*. Also frequently used for charter cruising, both the *Pushkin* and *Lermontov* also served on the North Atlantic. The 577ft-long *Pushkin* was laid-up in 1991 and then sold to the Orient Line and rebuilt as the cruise ship *Marco Polo*. She remains in service at the time of writing (2019).

Above right: Another transformation: having been the British troopship *Oxfordshire*, the ship was rebuilt as the *Fairstar*. (Mick Lindsay Collection)

Centre right: Italian sensations on the Australian run, the sister ships *Guglielmo Marconi* and *Galileo Galilei* were very popular with Italian and southern European migrants. (ALF Collection)

Below right: The Soviet *Alexandr Pushklin* off Tilbury – with the little Swedish liner *Britannia* off to the far left. (Mick Lindsay Collecion)

The greatly rebuilt *Achille Lauro*, arriving at Melbourne in February 1972. (Frank Andrews Collection)

ACHILLE LAURO

Another older liner thoroughly rebuilt and transformed into a new, sleek and almost unrecognisable form was Holland's *Willem Ruys* of 1947. After complete rebuilding in 1964–65, she reappeared as the *Achille Lauro*. Used on the Europe–Australia run, she later served as a popular cruise ship. Subject to a terrorist attack in October 1985, she had a sad ending: she burned and sank off East Africa in November 1994.

Another highly rebuilt liner: the *Angelina Lauro*, seen at Southampton, had been the *Oranje* of 1939. (Mick Lindsay Collection)

ANGELINA LAURO

The Lauro Line also bought another large Dutch liner, the *Oranje*, dating from 1939, and rebuilt it as the *Angelina Lauro*. She re-emerged in 1965. Like the previous *Achille Lauro*, she was barely recognisable. Also used in Europe–Australia service, she became a year-round cruise ship in 1972. She burned out at St Thomas in the US Virgin Islands on 30 March 1979 and then sank later that year while under tow and bound for the scrappers in Taiwan.

MICHELANGELO & RAFFAELLO

Big, very modern, and fast, these were also sadly the last Italian Line passenger ships. Completed in 1965, they were too late for profitable times on the run between Naples, Genoa, Cannes, Gibraltar and New York. Carrying 1,775 passengers in three classes, these 45,911-ton sisters were capped by unique lattice-style funnels and their amenities included no less than six swimming pools. Used in commercial service for only a decade, they were later sold to the Iranian Government for use as a moored military barracks – the *Michelangelo* at Bandar Abbas, the *Raffaello* at Bushire. The *Michelangelo* was scrapped in Pakistan in 1992; the *Raffaello* was sunk in an Iraqi missile attack in February 1983.

Above: Italian twins: the *Michelangelo* (left) and *Raffaello* together at New York in a view dated August 1973. (Author's Collection)

Left: Sweeping design: the *Raffaello* loading passengers at Naples. (Mick Lindsay Collection)

OCEANIC

Intended for seasonal North Atlantic service between Hamburg and Montreal, the ship's owners, the Home Lines, reconsidered plans, especially in view of increasing competition from air travel. Instead, the stunning new *Oceanic* was placed in year-round, seven-day cruise service between New York and Nassau. This 1,600-passenger ship was a huge success, carrying over 95 per cent of capacity in her first decade. Sold in 1985 to Premier Cruise Lines, she was renamed *Starship Oceanic*. Sold again, in 2000, to Pullmanturs (a Spanish cruise line), she then reverted to the name *Oceanic*. She began sailing for the Japanese-based Peace Boat Group until scrapped in China in 2012.

Right: The exteriors of both the *Michelangelo* and *Raffaello* were dominated by twin, lattice-work funnels. (Mick Lindsay Collection)

Below: Saturday-afternoon sailing: the *Oceanic* departs from New York – with the *Odessa, Rotterdam* and *Statendam* in the background – in this view dated June 1975. (Author's Collection)

SAGAFJORD

The new flagship of the Norwegian America Line, this ship was designed for seasonal Atlantic crossings, but in fact spent most of her life in cruising. Especially beautiful both inside and out, this 24,002-ton, French-built ship could carry a maximum of 789 passengers, but this number was often reduced to 500 to create a more intimate and luxurious atmosphere, ensuring a higher-quality passenger experience. Taken over by Cunard in 1983, she was later chartered out and sailed as the *Gripsholm*. Sold to UK-based Saga Cruises in 1997, she then sailed as the *Saga Rose* until 2009. Mostly laid-up from 2009, she was finally broken up in China in 2011.

EUGENIO C

She was the last three-class liner and the last to be built for the Italy–South America liner service. This 30,567-ton liner could carry up to 1,636 passengers and was the culmination of the Italian liner-building boom of the early 1960s. Renamed *Eugenio Costa* in 1984, she was by then used mostly for cruising. Sold to UK-based Lowline Cruises in 1996, she was renamed *Edinburgh Castle*. Sold again in 1999, she was now renamed *Big Red Boat II*. Laid-up from 2000, she finished her days when scrapped in India in 2005.

Above left: Near-sisters: the *Vistafjord* (left) and *Sagafjord* together at New York in December 1975. (Author's Collection)

Below left: Busy day at Genoa: the *Eugenio C* is in the foreground – with the *Carla C*, *Flavia* and *Enrico C* behind. (Costa Cruises)

World cruising: the handsome *Kungsholm* passes through the Panama Canal. (Mick Lindsay Collection)

KUNGSHOLM (1966)

A very handsome liner and one of the last to have twin funnels, the *Kungsholm* spent most of her career with the Swedish American Line as a luxury cruise ship. Built on the Clyde, this 26,678-ton liner was commissioned in the spring of 1966 and could carry up to 750 passengers. At first intended for seasonal Gothenburg–New York crossings, she spent most of her time cruising, carrying as few as 450 all first-class passengers. Sold to Flagship Cruises (Liberian flag) in

1975, she joined P&O Cruises (British flag) in 1978 and was rebuilt as the *Sea Princess*. Her forward 'dummy' funnel was removed during the refit and this marred the 660ft-long ship's otherwise handsome appearance. Renamed *Victoria* in 1995, she was sold in 2002 and later had various owners and different names: *Mona Lisa*, *Oceanic II* and *Veronica*. In her final career, she served as a floating hotel at Duqm in Oman until scrapped in India in 2015.

Pioneer cruise ship: the *Starward*, seen at San Juan in November 1983. (Author's Collection)

STARWARD

Sleek-looking and very contemporary, she and her near-sister *Skyward* were purposely built for cruising from Miami to the Caribbean. They were geared to the new age of mass-market cruising. Commissioned in 1968–69, the 12,949-ton *Starward* could carry up to 736 first -class passengers.

AMERIKANIS

Rebuilt from the Union–Castle Line's *Kenya Castle*, which dated from 1952, this ship was rebuilt by Chandris Lines and used primarily for cruises. During a major refit in 1967–68, the 17,041-ton ship's capacity was increased from 526 to 910.

In a photo dated 18 July 1987, the *Amerikanis* departs on a cruise to Bermuda – with Home Lines' then new *Homeric* to the left. (ALF Collection)

STEFAN BATORY

Holland America's *Maasdam* (q.v.) had a highly successful second career as Poland's *Stefan Batory*. She was used in service between Gdynia, other North European ports, London and also to Quebec City and Montreal. In winter, she made cruises.

Opposite: Departure day from Gdynia for the *Stefan Batory*. (ALF Collection)

Below: With a dominant funnel, West Germany's *Hamburg* later sailed as the *Maxim Gorky*. (Mick Lindsay Collection)

HAMBURG/MAXIM GORKY

Intended largely for long, luxurious cruises, the 600-passenger *Hamburg* of the German Atlantic Line was introduced in 1969 as 'the space ship'. The reference was to the high level of space per passenger on the 24,981-ton liner. Briefly renamed *Hanseatic* in 1973, her West German days were quite short-lived – she was soon sold to the Soviet-flag Black Sea Steamship Company and renamed *Maxim Gorky*.

QUEEN ELIZABETH 2

Commissioned to great interest, but also in uncertainty in May 1969, the *Queen Elizabeth 2* became the most successful big liner of all time. She carried more passengers, steamed more miles, visited more ports and made more money than other big liner. Her career spanned thirty-nine years. The 65,863grt, 963ft-long flagship of Cunard was designed to carry 2,005 passengers – 564 in first class and 1,441 in tourist. The *QE2* later served as a troopship during the Falklands War in 1982 and, in 1986–87, was converted to diesel drive. Retired in 2008, she was sold to Dubai-based buyers for use as a moored museum, hotel and residence. But the project was delayed until it finally opened in 2018.

This exceptional ship is a fitting end to the collection of liners featured in this book.

Above: Inaugural passage: the *Queen Elizabeth 2* passes through the Panama Canal for the first time in the spring of 1975. (Author's Collection)

Below: The *QE2* at New York's Pier 92 in this 1973 view – with the cruise ship *Sea Venture* to the left. (ALF Collection)

Right: The *QE2* glistening in lights while berthed at New York in this view from November 1969. (Author's Collection)

Below: The *QE2* was the most famous liner afloat when in service between 1969 and 2008. (ALF Collection)

BIBLIOGRAPHY

Dunn, Laurence, *Passenger Liners* (London: Adlard Coles Ltd, first edition, 1961).

Heine, Frank and Lose, Frank, *Great Passenger Ships of the World* (Hamburg: Koehlers Verlagsgesellschaft, 2010).

Kludas, Arnold, *Great Passenger Ships of the World*, 5 vols (Cambridge, England: Patrick Stephens Ltd, 1976–77).

Miller, William H., *Pictorial Encyclopedia of Ocean Liners, 1860–1994* (Mineola, New York: Dover Publications Inc., 1995).